"*Birdie, Give Me Your Heart* is a wonderful and inspiring story of how God's love and forgiveness can reach deep into our pain and suffering and bring healing to the very depths of our soul. All through the darkness and hurt, God in His mercy and grace brought angels into Birdie's life. These angels came to shine the light of Jesus and bring her hope in the midst of her cruel and desperate world. It is written in a tangible and purposeful way, showing us how to bring our damaged hearts to Jesus, the only One, who can heal our heart and set us free. Hooray for Birdie! Hooray for God!"

Gary and Marilyn Damron
Counselors and Seminar Speakers
Caring For The Heart Ministry

"God is in this! This story will have a great impact. There are so many people walking around with deep pain in their hearts because of having been abandoned and abused. *Birdie, Give Me Your Heart* offers such hope and healing. Upon reading this story, a person's response can only be, "If Birdie made it through all that and has found healing, then I can too." Jesus is clearly the answer as the story from Birdie's heart unfolds. Jesus knows the journey for each wounded heart to take that will arrive at a place of safety, healing and forgiveness. I highly recommend the reading of this book."

Ronna Grimes
Hope City Ministries, Kansas City , Kansas

"I am extremely touched by Birdie's story. Also, by the growth God has allowed Birdie to have in Him. *Birdie, Give Me Your Heart* will be a great help to people who have been through similar circumstances, but also will minister to those who have just been hurt through life's circumstances and have carried the hurt in their hearts far too long. I was intrigued by the part of the story that dealt with her healing. These steps will be extremely helpful to others who are seeking answers for their hurt."

Rod Brunson
Retired Publishing Agent
Longmont, Colorado

"*Birdie, Give Me Your Heart* is a powerful testimony to the eternal love story between Jesus Christ and Birdie. We have been privileged to be a part of Birdie's unique journey. Her honest sharing will give hope and encouragement to any who will choose as Birdie did, to risk giving their heart to Jesus."

Pastor Dave and Mrs. Cheryl ZumBrunnen
Wasilla, Alaska
Counselors and Workshop Leaders
True Life Counseling, Inc.

"From the first time I met Birdie, I recognized she was someone special. She had the quality of joy about her, a quality that while real, often hid the pain underneath. When I first heard part of Birdie's story, I knew that she had suffered more abuse than she realized. While physical abuse is traumatic, abandonment goes to the very soul of a child. What she witnessed being done to other children also peripherally traumatized her. Yet even knowing this, it was not until I read her book that I knew the depth of her suffering. No one comes through these experiences without being deeply scarred. Few overcome to the depth of healing that Birdie has reached. There is no doubt in my mind that she also has a peace that passes human understanding. I love you, Birdie."

Carol J. Elliot, M.S. L.P.C.
Anchorage, Alaska

Birdie,
GIVE ME YOUR HEART

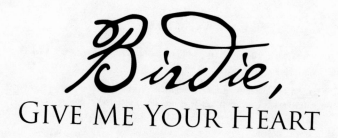

Birdie,
GIVE ME YOUR HEART

a true story by
ROBERTA PARRY

TATE PUBLISHING *&* Enterprises

Published by Tate Publishing & Enterprises, LLC
127 E. Trade Center Terrace | Mustang, Oklahoma 73064 USA
1.888.361.9473 | www.tatepublishing.com

Tate Publishing is committed to excellence in the publishing industry. The company reflects the philosophy established by the founders, based on Psalms 68:11,
"The Lord gave the word and great was the company of those who published it."

Book design copyright © 2008 by Tate Publishing, LLC. All rights reserved.
Cover design by Steven Jeffrey
Interior design by Janae J. Glass

Published in the United States of America

ISBN: 978-1-60462-929-3
1. Biography & Autobiography: Women   2. Family & Relationships: Abuse

08.04.14

I dedicate this book to Jeanie, Carolyn and Patricia,
my sisters and to the wounded hearts
of children performing today as adults.
My Child, Give Me Your Heart (Proverbs 23:26a).

ACKNOWLEDGMENTS

Dan Parry, my husband—you have been my knight in shining armor. You are the man of my dreams. Thank you for taking me on this adventure—for making me your bride, helpmeet, fishing partner, mother of your daughters, lover, and heart care partner. Thank you for caring for me through the forgiving of wounding memories. For being there during panic attacks and crying spells. Thank you for spreading your arms open wide and allowing Jesus to take over your life and live through you. You are more like Jesus than anyone I have ever met. Thank you with all my heart, my love.

My daughters—how precious you are to my heart! Thank you for the precious years I have been allowed to be your mother. You three have been the most important people in my life. God has used each of you in spectacular ways to reach and teach my heart. I so look forward to each day in the future that I get to spend with you.

Shelly, my firstborn—who you are delights me. I am so proud of your strength and loyalty. Thank you for your dear love and forgiveness. Thank you for calling me to share, whenever God answers your prayers. What a blessing you and Ryan are to dad and me. Thank you for the gift of our first grandchild. You are a wonderful mother to Kelsey Kaylene.

Tricia, my beautiful redhead—you have blessed me with your great love for animals, people, and for God. I have seen in you the gift of endurance. I believe you could be an Olympic Champion if you decided to become one. What a beautiful bride and helpmeet you are. Thank you for our first son-in-law, Nick. You are a woman after God's own heart. Thank you for your love and forgiveness.

Jessica, my beauty queen—the daughter who so reminds me of my own self. God used that likeness to speak into my wounded heart His healing. You brought a blanket of peace into our lives the day we brought you home as an infant. Now you are about to spread your wings and fly from our nest. God's blessing on your flight. May you land always in the palm of His hand. Thank you for your kisses and good-night hugs. They have been a healing balm to my heart. May Jesus touch others significantly through His life in you.

John and Barb Regier from Caring for the Heart Ministries— you both have brought to us the light at the end of the tunnel. You did as Jesus suggested in the story of the Good Samaritan. You stopped along the wayside to help those wounded and left to die. Thank you for stopping for Dan and me. Our hearts are forever grateful for your love, care, and friendship. Through your caring ministry, many hearts have been retrieved, healed, and given back to the wonderful God we call Father. From our hearts to yours, thank you.

Dave and Cheryl ZumBrunnen, my friends—more than anyone, you both have covenanted with me through the turmoil of my confusion and darkness. You brought me the truth of who God truly is and His purpose for the Life He has given me. Thank you for bringing me to the cross. To the cross I will cling, for therein I found True Life.

Grandma Carol—you have been in my life for twenty-seven years. Always there, just a phone call away. Someone I have always been able to talk with, share my heart with, and receive no judgment—just a listening heart. You have blessed my life with your unconditional love and been a special grandma to my three daughters. Thank you for loving me and not wanting to change me into someone you thought I should be.

Mary Taylor—thank you for your interest in me and my life. You have encouraged me throughout this whole process. Especially by allowing me to take my beginner steps in counseling by letting me try them out on you. That takes a person who really believes in me and is willing to take a risk herself. Thank you for the sewing machine. Thank you for every one of those holiday cards with *moolah* that you sent my daughters. Your attention toward them has been a balm to my heart.

Gary and Marilyn Damron, our closest heart-to-heart friends—thank you. Friends like you make all the difference in the world. You have gone with us through not only the joys, but also the sorrows of the heart. You have blessed us with your tenderness and generosity of time. Together, we've been Regiered.

My Father God—thank You for pursuing me with Your love. Thank You for knowing all that I have been through and understanding why I am who I am. Thank You for sending Your Son to capture my heart and give up His life to purchase mine. Thank You for never giving up on me, instead picking me up from the heap of my broken dreams. You are the one I look to and ask, "What do You think about this?" I know that I can come running to You and sit in Your lap; we can visit and You will share with me Your heart. Thank You for choosing me to be Your daughter. I love You, Daddy, with all my heart.

Jesus, my brother, friend, savior, shepherd, comfort, and my life. Thank You for coming to rescue me. Thank You for leading the way back home. Thank You for being right there with me through all the abandonment and abuse. Come, live Your life through me, touching others with the love of God. Thank You for being my hero. "For this purpose was the Son of God manifested, that He might destroy the works of the devil" (I John 3:8).

TABLE OF CONTENTS

FOREWORD

When I was asked to share a word about a book describing the struggles Birdie and Dan went through, it was easy to say yes. Yes, due to the excitement I have experienced as a pastoral counselor observing them come to freedom from the pain of their past. God did a miraculous work in their lives, for which I am grateful to God.

I remember the two weeks that Birdie and Dan spent in my office. They came damaged and wounded from their past emotional pain. The high level of pain Birdie experienced from her abandonment and abuse motivated me to want to help her and others like her come to freedom. I have known Birdie and Dan for only five years, but seeing God transform their lives, releasing them from pain, and then seeing them reach out to help other people who were struggling has caused me to have a great appreciation for them.

Birdie, Give Me Your Heart is really about God's faithfulness to a girl who has been severely damaged. God's desire to accept and care for each person is clearly revealed as Birdie goes through life being taken away or left behind, from one mother after another, from one dad after another. Each new set of parents brought a new set of rules causing her to be continually confused. God faithfully sent *angels*, individuals who cared for her at each period in her life, until she was able to understand and resolve each of the painful areas of her past.

As you read the story of Birdie, I would ask that you evaluate the pain from your past and ask Jesus to heal and bring peace to your pain. I trust this book will encourage you to take your emotional pain to Jesus and experience His touch to take the pain from your heart. The prayers and steps that Birdie took can be followed by any person seeking to find freedom from their past pain.

I would ask you to pray that God would lead you to a friend who has been damaged, to share with them the steps they can follow to come to freedom from their pain. The process of healing from one's pain can be accomplished through leading one in prayer to Jesus who is the Wonderful Counselor and the only one that can truly heal damaged hearts.

My prayer is that this book will touch many lives and hearts, bringing them closer to a caring and loving Father who desires to understand, accept, and care about their pain and bring them to freedom.

With thanksgiving to the Lord Jesus Christ,
John Regier, Director
Caring For The Heart Ministry
www.caringfortheheart.com, design, A Tier One, 2006

INTRODUCTION

"Give Me thy heart," says the Father above—
No gift so precious to Him as our love;
Softly He whispers wherever thou art,
"Gratefully trust Me and give Me thy heart."
"Give Me thy heart," says the Saviour of men,
Calling in mercy again and again;
"Trust in Me only, I'll never depart—
Have I not died for thee? Give Me thy heart."
"Give Me thy heart," says the Spirit divine;
"All that thou hast to My keeping resign;
Grace more abounding is Mine to impart—
Make full surrender and give Me thy heart."
"Give Me thy heart, give Me thy heart"
Hear the soft whisper, wherever thou art;
From this dark world He would draw thee apart,
Speaking so tenderly, "Give Me thy heart."
Words: Eliza E. Hewitt, 1898, (Public Domain)

One morning I was awakened by this song being sung to me. I knew that my Father in Heaven was speaking to my heart. His desire was to draw me from the dark world I found myself in and to set me free from abusive damage that had been done to my heart. My name is Birdie. I am writing this book so that the world may know that God and Jesus are real and active in our lives here on earth. I don't have all the answers. But I have come into contact with the One who does. Contact with God has healed my heart of damage. Damage so great that my heart died and I buried it, hoping to never feel pain again. One day God impressed on me to give my dead heart to Him. I didn't have a use for my broken heart, so I handed my heart over. This is the story of how my heart got damaged and broken and the incredible healing process God took me through.

Who God is was misconstrued to me due to the abuse I went through as a child. Abuse caused by people who said they knew and walked with God. Consequently, I lived out my life with a wrong concept of God and who I was in relationship to Him. I also had people come into my life, who I like to call my *angels*. I will refer to them as *angels* when they appear in my story. I call them *angels* because they brought light into my darkness. These individuals brought light filled with love, which remained within me and gave me hope to go on in the darkness. These people inwardly had the love of God and outwardly wooed me to look upward to a God I didn't know truly existed. Jesus is the Hero of my story. It was He who brought me into relationship with a loving God, whom I now call Heavenly Father.

My First Memories
of Childhood

A beautiful brunette woman drove the car. I cannot remember her name or why I was with her. I sat on the front seat of the car as we pulled up in the driveway of a white house. On the porch was a heavy woman sitting in a porch swing with a large, brown teddy bear. The brunette woman came around, lifted me out of the car, took me onto the porch, and set me down in front of the woman with the bear. The teddy bear was offered to me, but all of a sudden I became afraid. I knew instinctively that I was being offered the teddy bear as a form of trickery. I reached for the woman I knew; as I did so, the woman on the swing grabbed me and hung onto me. I turned my head and began to scream, crying out as I watched the brunette woman walk away quickly and get into her car. I reached my arms and hands out toward her, screaming, as she drove the car out of my sight. To this day, I have no idea who that woman was. She may have been my real mother. I do not know. I was eighteen months old when this occurred in my life. The woman with the teddy bear was my first foster mother, whom I lived with for one year and a half. I do not remember any more about living in this home during this time. However, I did return to this same home later in my childhood.

My next memory occurs on a farm with a tall man and his wife. I hardly remember the woman; the man looms in my memory. They had a small child of their own. There was a big dog we were scared of, a huge bull, and lots of mud on the farm. My two older sisters, whom I came to understand later were my real sisters, lived with me there. My oldest sister was chased by the bull one day while trying to get to the school bus. I remember that the foster home was a very fearful place. I have one good memory of an Easter morning, getting to look for a basket and finding one that was all my own. It was hidden behind the overstuffed rocking chair. My life felt dark and scary there. I was glad to leave.

In the next year, my younger sister was born; sometime after her first birthday, she and I were placed in a wonderful foster home. At the time I had no idea who this other little girl was, but came to know from the conversation of the adults around me, that she was my little sister. I think they must have owned an apple orchard. There were three sons. They all slept upstairs in a bedroom together. The mother used to let me go wake up the boys in the morning by jumping up and down on their beds until they woke up. This woman and her husband wanted to adopt my younger sister and me. The court system would not allow us to be adopted without adopting my two older sisters, and we were soon taken away from those who wanted us. I remember laughter and fun while living here in this home. I tucked this little bit of light away in my heart. My two other sisters were at this time living with my oldest sister's school teacher.

I was four years old when my three sisters and I were moved into my fourth foster home. It was again the home of the woman with the teddy bear. The man drove a truck that had the letters RX on the side, and he went to work in it every day. The woman stayed at the house with us. They had sons of their own; one son was my age. We lived here for the next four years. There were ten of us foster children. We all slept upstairs in a room with four beds. Whenever I was in trouble, I slept on a hard plastic bed down in a dark basement. It was scary to sleep down there all alone. However, I do remember a streetlight coming in the small basement window. Breakfast usually consisted of a slice of bread in a glass of milk or a bowl of cold cereal on Sundays. For lunches, we came home from school and ate a hot dog or a sandwich. I never remember eating a supper meal in this foster home. We may have, I just cannot remember ever eating any meals in the evening time. The fostered children never were permitted to sit on the furniture. We always sat on the floor. I was never hugged or embraced in any way while living in this home.

My younger sister and I wet the bed most every night. In the morning, if we were wet, we had to sit on the bottom step of the stairs, which led up to our bedroom, until it was time to go to school. We went to school hungry. In kindergarten, all the children received a carton of milk during recess. I loved this milk. I was so disappointed when I got to first grade; we had to pay ten cents for the milk. So I had to watch all the kids who could afford ten cents every day drink my beloved milk. One day I found a dime on the floor and turned it in for milk. That was perhaps the best glass of milk I've ever had. Today, I never pass up a dime I see on the ground—it always brings that milk to my mind.

I was hungry all the time. Due to a hamburger joint down the street we lived on, people would throw out their leftovers as they drove down our block. My younger sister and I would pick up these leftovers on the way home from our elementary school and eat them. This is how we survived not being fed. I would sometimes get up in the middle of the night to eat the leftovers I could find on the table from the foster family's supper meal. One morning after having done this, the foster mother told us that she had put a chocolate laxative in the food in order to catch whoever was stealing the food. It did not work on me, though, because I never did have to go to the bathroom that day. I think my body was so malnourished it just enjoyed the chocolate laxative.

At school, I stole from lunch boxes left by students in the coat closet. I would find some excuse for going in there and tucked food in my underwear until I could go to the bathroom and enjoy. One day, I put the leftovers in a desk I sat in, but then had to change classrooms for a different school subject. The schoolteachers found out I had been stealing the food from the lunch boxes. But they could never make me confess to the crime. I was too afraid of the beating I might get from the foster dad.

The foster dad often beat us with his belt. He would make us lie on our backs on the floor, putting our heads between his feet. He would then proceed to whip us with his belt. We were hit wherever the belt landed as he swung. Sometimes he made us take all our clothes off first. One whipping occured when I had a boil—which happened a lot when I was a child—and blood went everywhere as it popped. The blood scared him badly, and the spanking ended for the night. I remember him tying my little sister and me to the bedposts at night when we got into trouble for playing whenever we were supposed to be sleeping.

Very special *angels* came to us while we lived in this foster home. First was the police officer who helped us cross the busy street on our way to school. Every day we walked to school, he was there to see that we safely got across the busy street. He was always kind and smiled. He sometimes would take my hand while we crossed over. He was tall in my eyes. His name was Andy. I am crying as I write this; my heart is touched that I have never forgotten his name after all these years—even though I was only five years old at the time. He showed me that warmth and kindness were present in this world.

Church *angels*, people from local churches, brought two new swing sets for us to play on. We spent many times laughing and playing on those swings and slides. The gift of a swing set was a beam of light to my heart that told me goodness was present in this world.

One Christmas morning, an *angel* in a long red coat came to our house with a big box of presents. I was sitting on the bottom step of the stairs—I had wet the bed that morning. She came with three other people to hand out Christmas presents to us foster children. I was not receiving any, because I had to stay on the step until the foster mom said I could get up. I was distraught; I knew I would be left out and not given a present. But at the bottom of the box of presents, the lady in the red coat found a baby doll. By some miracle, she looked up, glanced in my direction, and motioned for me to come receive the doll. I quickly glanced over at the foster mom for the okay to move. She shook her head yes, and I bounded over to get my hands on that baby doll. She didn't have any clothes on her; she was just a used doll passed on to GoodWill. But I soon found something to wrap her in. The lady in the red coat hugged me, and to this day I believe she said, "Jesus loves you." I love old baby dolls because they remind me of that happy memory. I later gave the doll away to a missionary to take to an orphan girl in Africa. It was a gift of love from my heart; it was truly hard for me to part with that doll.

I knew about Jesus and that Christmas day was when He had been born. Once in a while I got to go to Sunday School, and I learned the chorus "Jesus Loves Me." I did not know what that word *love* meant, but the song was a happy song, and I loved to sing about Jesus. We did a program at school also about Baby Jesus, and by some big chance I got to hold the baby during the play and rock Jesus to sleep. Of course, it was only a doll.

My kindergarten teacher was Miss Angel. No kidding. She too was one of my *angels*. She would let me hold her hand and walk slowly with her during recess. I loved holding her hand and walking with her. She never made me go play on the days I just wanted to stay with her. Three-fourths of the way through the school year, she resigned her job because she was getting married. She was a ray of sunshine in my life, helping me to see gentleness somewhere in my dark world.

One day I was walking to school with the other children. The older children began to call out that there was a witch who lived in the little brown house. They said we should throw rocks at her windows and break them. I was five at the time, and, having listened to the story of Hansel and Gretel, I was afraid of a witch living near me. I picked up the largest rock I could find and threw it at one of her windows. I must have had a good pitching arm, because the window broke with a loud crash. Out of the house came a tiny woman with long, white hair who could not speak because she was mute. I ran off as fast as I could to school. Later in the day, I was called to the principal's office. The woman had come to the school and communicated to the principal about what had happened to her window. All the children that had walked with me to school told the principal I had thrown the rock. I was in big trouble. I simply told the truth, which was that I was scared of the witch who lived there. The principal kindly told me that the kids had lied to me and that she was not a witch. Other children from the foster home had also told him how much trouble I would get into if he told the foster parents what I had done. They told him about the punishments I would get. He assured me that I would not be spanked. I did not believe him. But he must have given them a good talking to; when I fearfully went home, the foster parents were very nice to me. They took me out to eat a meal, where they told me I would have to tell the lady I was sorry and give her money for a new window. When I got there, the lady was nice; she gave me two cookies with milk. I would not eat the cookies or drink the milk as I still believed she was a witch and thought she had poisoned them. I remembered how the witch in the story had been nice to the children to begin with and only became evil later. The woman could not talk either, and this made me very afraid of her. I am sure she was a very nice lady and probably would have been another *angel*, if I had only gotten to know her.

My worst memory of living in this foster home, was the time they threatened to send me away. I had done something wrong, and they shut me up in a dark stairwell. This terrified me; the older children had told me that a dragon lived at the top of the stairwell. They even showed me his footprints out in our backyard. They were huge. I sat on the stairwell all Friday, kicking and screaming until they told me that on the next Monday, someone was coming to take me to a different home. This shut me up. I was terrified of being taken anywhere. I did not want to leave what I knew; even though it was miserable, it was safe—it was the only home I knew. So, for the next three days, I was quiet. I did not make a sound. On Monday morning, they did not let me go to school because, supposedly, I was leaving that day. Halfway into the day, they asked me, "If we give you another chance, and let you stay, will you be good?" Well, of course I had no idea of how to be good, I didn't even know how I was being bad, but I shook my head in a vigorous nod. I was relieved, happy even, that I was getting to stay. I tried to be good. Good to me was being quiet and staying out of the way.

My favorite memory was when we all got to sit in the front room and watch the dramatic movie version of *Cinderella* with real actors. This drama and story enabled my little heart to believe that even though my life was dark and scary, someday my prince would come and rescue me. Someday...

THE CHILDREN'S HOME

A photographer came to our house and took a picture of my three sisters and me. We got to sit on the couch to take the picture. I had never sat on the couch before this moment, so I felt special.

Less than a month later, we four girls were told that we would be moving away to another children's home. I didn't believe them; they had told me this before and it didn't happen. The day arrived, though, and they packed us up with one change of clothing and our few toys and drove us ten hours away to another home. We stopped at a roadside cafeteria to eat lunch; none of us ate much of our food. We had plates full of fried chicken, mashed potatoes, peas, and a roll. We had never seen so much food before. We were so scared about where we were going and what was going to happen to us, we couldn't swallow but a few bites. The waitress could not believe we would not eat all that good food. The foster mom told her what was happening to us that day. The sweet waitress took the peas away and brought us dishes of ice cream. Even this treat could not cheer us up or cause the fear to go away.

When we arrived at the home, we got out of the car. The one brown box containing all of our belongings was pulled out of the trunk and set onto the ground. Several people were there to welcome us, but we clung to the foster mother. We cried very loudly as the people pulled our hands off of her dress. She cushioned her leaving by telling us she would visit us. I never saw her again, though I kept looking for her to come for a long time.

The children's home was Christian-faith based. It was started by good-hearted people who intended to provide proper care for children who did not have homes. There were several houses, each housing twelve to fourteen children. The children were cared for by a married couple they called mom and pop or dad. The children attended school on campus until high school, at which time they went to a local high school in town. All the families ate meals together in a large building called the dining hall. They called us to eat by ringing a large bell outside, which could be heard from all the houses. Each family had their own long or circular table where they sat to eat. Each child had a job to do after the meal to help clean up the dining hall. I remember the first meal we ate there. Breakfast was a pile of scrambled eggs, sausage, pancakes, and all the orange juice and milk we could drink. We were in heaven. I finally experienced what it meant to be so full that I did not want to eat any more.

My first set of parents at the home were around twenty-one years of age. They were young for the job of parenting twelve children ranging from six to eighteen years of age. My pop was very tall and had long arms. My mom was short and very pretty. They had a young son of their own. My pop's parents were also parents at the home, so we had "grandparents." His mother cut my sisters' and my hair the day we arrived, which made us very upset. She was very nice, though, and gave us coloring books and crayons afterward. I loved the red crayon the best. My pop's sister was also a house parent with her husband, so we also had an "aunt and uncle." All our families got together for watermelon and ice cream socials. It was great fun. We would spit the watermelon seeds behind our house down a hill; later we had watermelons growing up out of the ground. Many happy times occurred in this home, and these stories need to be shared before the unhappy ones. Both the good and the bad affected my life and heart.

My mom loved to sing; as we drove places, she taught us many gospel choruses. My favorite was a song we sang in rounds about loving Jesus. I grew to love singing because of how happy we all were when we sang. This woman placed within my heart a melody and a desire to sing, which in later years gave me strength during my emotional breakdown. We always would gather in the living room as a family for devotions. This was a time for reading out of the Holy Bible and praying to God before bedtime. We all sat on the floor and listened as pop read to us. We loved these times.

My pop used to play hide-and-seek with us. He could hide in the most awesome places, and we would never see him. Then he would jump out and scare us silly. We would squeal and run away as fast as we could to hide from him. He built a go-cart that we had so much fun sitting in and pretending we were driving. He hung a thick, long rope up in a tree upon which we would climb up and swing far out over the hill. I also loved the challenge of climbing up to the top of this rope.

After we were at the home for a couple of months, a couple from another state began to sponsor my three sisters and myself with the support of their church. They brought us a new swing set and seven new dresses that the ladies of the church had sewn for us. These ladies were *angels*. I had only owned one dress before. I felt like a princess. They also made matching dresses for us four girls. We got a lot of attention when we wore those dresses. We loved the attention. We were starved for attention.

At the age of eight I decided I wanted to accept Jesus as my Savior and be baptized. I did not understand then all of what that meant; I only knew that Jesus was the Son of God sent as a man by God to be my Savior. Something extraordinary happened the night I went forward in my church to tell everyone I wanted Jesus as my Savior. It is a memory that I will always treasure. I had gone forward in the church service and told everyone that I believed Jesus was the Son of God, and that I was accepting Him as my

Savior. As I turned around to go back to my family, my house grandpa was there right behind me, kneeling on the floor. He had tears in his eyes, and he embraced me in his big arms with a bear hug. He said, "Birdie, I am so proud of you." He hugged me and wouldn't let me go. This is the first  embracing hug I remember getting in my life. I felt so loved and cherished. Later in my life, during an emotional crisis, I asked God where and when He had been there for me. He reminded me of this moment and said to my heart, "I was inside this man, and I was embracing you that day, welcoming you as my daughter. I was saying, through him, how proud I was of you for receiving my free gift of salvation. I was crying through this man, because with the faith of a little child you were believing I existed and coming to me, your Father."

With the good also came the bad. My first spanking came one day when I had walked out of the house, going to  what I thought was the front yard where there were swing sets and slides to play on. My house mom came out of the house carrying a paddle. She was upset and told me that I could not leave the yard without permission and I was going to get a spanking. I was so shocked, as I did not know the boundaries of where the yard was, and I had never heard of this rule before this moment. I was being punished for doing wrong, although I was not intentionally trying to go where I was not supposed to go. She did not give me a chance to respond to the charges. Then and there I decided in my heart that I had better figure out what all the rules were so I would not get spanked. Punishment was painful, and I did not like the pain it inflicted on my body. Besides I wanted to be a good girl, not bad. This vow I took in my heart later caused huge consequences in my life as I tried to keep all the rules and uphold standards in order to stay away from punishment.

My youngest sister and I continued to wet the bed. Several nights my house parents dressed us only in diapers and made us crawl on our hands and knees through the living room while the other kids were told to laugh at us and call us babies. They did this thinking it would correct the bed-wetting problem. They did not realize that it was a heart issue. I would then climb into bed humiliated and cry myself to sleep. I began to hide my diapers behind the dresser. Then I would give my house mom a dry one the next morning. She would be so proud and happy with me. I liked the love she gave me when I produced what she wanted. We ran out of diapers eventually, and one day my mom smelled something very strong in my room. She found the diapers; I was once again shamed and whipped with a paddle for punishment. That acceptance had been short lived. I was sad, because I had no idea how to stop wetting the bed or I would have done anything to stop. It was not within my power.

In fact, my wetting the bed did not stop until the day I gave birth to my first daughter, when I was twenty-four-years-old. I believe when I went to sleep, I really did not want to wake up again due to the trauma in my life. I went into a very deep sleep from which I could not wake up when my bladder was needing release. After giving birth, I now had a reason to live, because I now belonged to someone and someone belonged to me. This prognosis is given by me, not from medical knowledge but from my own personal heart and life experience. These parents got in contact with me years later and asked me to forgive them. They realized how young they had been to be put in such a house of responsibility. They had no understanding of how to nurture wounded children. We have established a very loving relationship, and they actually helped begin the process of the healing of my heart. They opened a door to the first counselor who helped me get in touch with the damage done to my heart as a child.

After two years of living with these house parents, they— along with their parents, sister, and her husband—decided  to leave the children's home due to a disagreement with the leadership about bringing juvenile delinquents, who had been in trouble with the law, into the home to live with young, abandoned, and orphaned children. Consequently, out of my life went a support group of people who had become my family. I had no emotion about them leaving. My heart was cold on their departure day. My immediate thought was, "Oh well, I will not be staying here for long. We will be moving soon." I thought this because we had never stayed anywhere very long. What I didn't realize was that my nightmare here was just beginning. I would not wake up from it for a very long time.

HOUSE OF FEAR & PUNISHMENT

I was not yet ten years of age when my sisters and I moved into a different house with a new set of house parents at the children's home. The house dad was known by all the children to be very strict and mean. When I heard whose house we were being moved into, I immediately was afraid. This fear became a nightmare in which no child should ever have to live. The trauma I experienced in this house caused me to walk in fear for a very long period of my life.

My housemother was very kind; in her own way she showed me lots of care and love. Mom sewed clothes for me that I adored. She allowed me to watch her lay the pattern on the material and cut out the outfit she was making. I was allowed to stand beside her and watch the sewing process of the outfit from beginning to end. I learned to love sewing and creating because of the time she allowed me to stay at her side. I later would sew all my clothes in high school, due to the fact that all our clothes came from a used-clothing storehouse. The only way I had new clothes to wear as a teenager was to make them myself. This *angel* gave me a precious gift of time and creativity, which caused a ray of self-esteem and respect to shine into my heart.

My housefather was a totally different story. He was a

preacher at a local church in the community. He did not allow girls to wear jeans or trendy clothing. Whenever the long maxi dresses, which were quite modest, became popular, we could not wear even them. Our blouses always had to go lower than our bottoms when we wore slacks. A television was not allowed in our home. He was outwardly a very conservative Christian. He was tough and strong. He took care of the horses the home owned. He loved to fish and hunt. I went on many of the fishing trips with him. He had the responsibility of keeping all the homes in firewood as we heated our houses with fireplaces.

I can't even remember the first time he spanked me. I do remember how he spanked us. He used a long, wide, wooden board. He made us get down on all fours beside a bed and put our heads on the floor and our bottoms in the air to spank us. If we made a sound, he would add five more swats to what he was already dishing out. I usually got ten swats, but the most I ever counted him giving me was twenty-five. I was only a little girl, but I never made a sound while he was spanking me. There were several reasons for the spankings. Always at report card time, we got five swats for a D grade and ten swats for an F grade. We all lived in fear of report card time. Of course, my grades were horrible, and the notes from the teachers about me were all about my misconduct during class. My teachers never knew or took into consideration the trauma I had already been through or the horror I was living through now. There was no way I could function academically and learn very well. I was just trying to survive each and every day—physically and emotionally.

Once, my sister and I were made to stand up in the living room half the night until one of us confessed to putting dirty panties back in the clean panty drawer. We both were finally spanked and put to bed. I went to sleep every night trying to figure out what I could have done that day to deserve a spanking from him. I lived in constant fear of doing something wrong and being punished.

One traumatic evening, after taking a shower, I came into my bedroom with a bathrobe wrapped around me. I had just gotten a new game for Christmas, and the girls were on the bed playing with it without my permission. I started yelling at them. I rarely had anything of my very own, and when I did get something, I was very possessive. All of a sudden I was hit from behind with a belt. There was dad, hitting me with his belt over and over again. By the time he was done, I was sitting on the floor with my bathrobe completely undone. I was shaking, humiliated, and in shock of what I had just endured. He then told all of us girls to get to the living room for devotions. I wrapped my bathrobe around myself and went to sit in the living room to listen to him read out of the Holy Bible for twenty minutes. The next morning when he saw the welts and stripes on my legs from my heel to the middle of my thigh, he told me to wear leotards to school until every mark disappeared. I did what he told me and never told anyone or showed anyone. I did fantasize that someone would accidentally see the marks and rescue me. I was too traumatized by fear to show anyone.

Once after he spanked me with his horse's double-belted whip, I decided to go to the office and show someone. To help me gain the courage to go, I told my sister. Out of fear for her own survival, she told on me. Dad ordered me to his bedroom and was going to spank me again. I begged and begged him to not hit me again. My housemother was in the bedroom at the time, but she was ill. It was a Sunday, and he needed to get to church. He let me off with a terrifying warning of what would happen if I ever thought about going to the office again. This same man stood in the pulpit on Sundays and preached messages about God. I was actually inspired by his sermons. I didn't know then that the word of God was inspiring me, not the man.

In their home they had Bible storybooks. I read many stories out of these books. Through them I came to learn about the God of the Old Testament. I read the stories of Esther, David and Goliath, Daniel in the lion's den, Joseph, and Noah. I read about Jesus and the healing that he brought to people after many years of sickness. I loved these stories and thought to myself, "This God is pretty powerful and awesome." I believed these stories were true and that God was real. Later, Jesus gave me a picture that He had been holding me in his lap as I read these stories. Those stories gave me hope in a God who could one day help me.

My dad had inappropriate relationships with the teenage girls in our home. When a new teenage girl would move into our home, he would begin to make her his favorite. All of us girls saw it and knew what was going on with him. Out of fear, we never talked about what was happening. He uncovered himself once in front of me in my bedroom when I was home sick from school. I turned my face to the wall in embarrassment. He tickled me, trying to get me to turn around. The phone rang, and he had to leave my room to answer a call from the office. Another providential moment. In this house were two teenage boys who would take my little sister and me to a van and touch us inappropriately. This happened to me about six times before the boys left the children's home. At this age, I did not know that what they were doing to me was wrong; I did not realize how my innocence and childhood were being stolen from me. My house dad and mom would hug us occasionally when we were saying goodnight. It was during this that my dad would ask me if I loved him; when I fearfully would answer yes, he would tell me to show him how much. I would quickly give him another kiss on the cheek and run off to bed. I would get under my blankets and scoot as far down as I could in bed, as if my blankets could keep me safe. To this day, if I am having an anxiety attack, a blanket wrapped around me causes me to feel secure.

This house dad once dared my sister who was eight to grab hold of an electric fence and he would give her a dollar. She did it, but she could not let go of the fence because of the strength of the shock against her small body. Someone had to turn off the fence's power. His own son even got run over by a horse after he told us to make a circle around  some wild horses. The wildest mare picked the smallest person to run over, and it happened to be his little boy. Once, I fell off a horse, and he switched me until I climbed back on. He used the fear of punishment to make us not be afraid of anything else. I watched him switch a young man all the way to school one day. He ran behind him, hitting him with a large stick. The young man was humiliated, and I was a witness to the humiliation on his face as they ran past me on our way to school. I hated this man and would have killed him if I could have turned my fear into courage.

I was just one of the many kids they watched over, making us be good and act proper in public. This was a ministry to them. They got honor in the church for being missionaries and giving up all for God. It was the pride of a so-called godly life. The better we behaved, the better they looked. They controlled us into good behavior through fear of punishment. It was not good behavior because of respect and love for the parent. All the kids did many things behind the parents' backs. It was easy. There were so many kids, they could not keep track of what was going on all the time. The kids knew when those times were and that they could get away with whatever they wanted to do. They did not have our hearts; therefore they did not have our true obedience, respect, or trust.

I remember one of my sisters was very sick from appendicitis; this dad refused to take her to the hospital. She was bent over all day and was forced to go to church. My sister became so ill, they were forced to take her to the hospital. By the time she arrived there, the doctors did not know if she would pull through. They never took us to the doctor; it would be in my adulthood, when I was about to marry, when I went to a real doctor for the first time. The home hired a school nurse who would give us our prescription medicines and shots. They did not call her until we were very sick. I was so sick once, I fainted from a 104-degree fever; they finally brought in the nurse to give me an antibiotic shot. I had tonsillitis and strep throat combined.

Two of my worst memories involved one of my sisters. One day, she and I were arguing in the back of the work truck while we were helping unload a pile of wood at one of the houses. All of a sudden, dad told us to get out of the truck and run two miles back to where we had gotten the wood in the forest. He said, "You need to get there before I do with the truck or I am going to switch you." We both ran as fast as our little legs could carry us. The whole way, I could hear my sister calling out my name, begging me to wait for her. I was in such fear of being switched that I did not stop for her. I have hurt and cried with grief over this—my failure to stop and help my own sister. By some luck, dad did not switch us when we finally got there. He just laughed and told us to get to work piling the brush from the fallen trees.

The second worst memory is that one day when our house dad came to my sister and me to tell us that one of us was going to be put in another home. He said, "I am going to make the decision over the next month. So whichever one of you behaves the best, I am going to keep." Well, I cried, prayed out to God in fear, and pleaded with Him to not let me be sent away. Even though I lived in fear in this home, I was more afraid of being sent away and the changes of people in my life. It traumatized me to think of what could happen somewhere else. Well, God answered my prayer, or so it seemed at the time. The day came that I had to watch my sister being taken away from all she knew—

and her three sisters—to a new home. My fear then turned into guilt and shame for the pain I imagined she was going through. I found out later that they moved her in with a teacher in order to help her in school.

Some *angels* came along during this period of my life. First, there was a lady cook who took me into her home. She taught me all kinds of crafts, such as embroidery, how to cover hangers, and hand sewing. She let me come to her house on Saturdays and work with her all afternoon. I loved going there, and I found out that I was capable of learning and making beautiful creations. She taught me patience and goodness. She left in my heart a ray of sunshine that helped me survive in those dark days.

College kids would come every so often and work at the school on projects. These kids would love all over us children. They would play with us, hold us on their laps, and talk with us. We cried and clung to them when they had to leave to go back to school. We desperately wanted to go with them.

My sixth and seventh grade teacher would read wonderful classic novels to us. I loved these stories; they were about children who finally won after many trials. They gave me the hope of something good one day coming into my life. This *angel* taught me a love for reading and writing. She made me want to be a good speller. She rewarded our good work while never causing us to feel bad whenever we failed. She always baked us a cake for our birthdays. I remember the cake she made for me one birthday. It was a treat out of heaven to me.

Then there were my sponsors. People in churches would pick a child to sponsor at the home. My *angel* sponsors sent me a beautiful purple bicycle. I was ten years old. My goals in life were to learn to ride a bicycle and how to whistle. I worked and worked until I accomplished riding that bike, although I didn't learn to whistle until I was eighteen. My mouth just couldn't pucker right.

Another *angel* was a new girl who came to the home with her real parents. Her parents were to be the house parents in the home next door to us. She was a pretty redhead, and she came with a purple bicycle just like mine. We quickly became best friends. We walked to school together every day. Her mother sent me a piece of mint gum every day. My friend provided me much joy and love. We enjoyed playing, talking, and riding our bikes. We never argued or got upset with each other. Her friendship was the calm in the midst of a storm. The day came, though, that her parents decided to move, which broke my heart with grief. But, she did leave a ray of light in my heart that enabled me to walk on toward the future.

My house mom and house dad both had mothers who would come to visit us from time to time. One grandmother would come on the train. She was tall, thin, and stylish. She would bring the most wonderful peanut butter fudge. Once the train was in a wreck, so she could not go home from her visit with us. We children were all so glad she had to stay two weeks longer. Our house dad did not spank us while she was there. The other grandmother was short, full bodied, and always wore an apron. She brought wonderful cookies with her. She also would make us the best homemade noodles I have ever tasted. We loved for these *angels* to come visit.

Finally the day came when these parents were actually asked to leave. We kids did not know this until years later.

They went on a vacation, so they could find a new job. When they returned, their children were not with them. When we asked where the children were, they told us that they were leaving the home for good and had left the children with their grandparents. I was secretly glad that this dad was leaving. I was so happy that I would never be spanked by him again. I was so cold toward him in my heart. But, my house mom was a different story. I could not believe she was leaving me. On top of that, they chose to take a teenage girl with them, who I knew was in an inappropriate relationship with the house dad. I was so bitter and in shock that they would take her and not us four sisters with them. We had lived with them longer, and my heart did not understand why they chose her over us. I was thirteen at the time. Even though it seemed like heaven that they were leaving, the abandonment and rejection hit me like a ton of bricks. It left a tremendous emotional wound in my heart and soul. To top it all off, I found out that the home had decided to move my two older sisters into other homes. They would be leaving me all by myself. All my sisters were eventually moved to different states to separate children's homes. Just when I didn't think it could get any worse, something unthinkable or unimaginable would happen in my life. No one ever sat down with me and explained anything. I was left to adjust on my own, with no understanding except what I learned through listening to people talk around me or my own childish perceptions of the situations.

A Bitter & Unresponsive Heart

The dining hall bell rang; we were headed for lunch when a large moving truck pulled up to the playground. A man with sunglasses got out of the truck and came around to open the truck door for a woman holding a baby boy. We were expecting a new set of house parents to arrive any day. These people were to be my new mom and dad. I didn't care. I was not open to any new parents or people coming into my life. My heart was closed to new relationships, and I was determined not to open it up to anyone. I hated them before they even arrived. Of course, they had no idea of who this young, thirteen-year-old girl was they were getting as a daughter in their home. They had no idea how cold my heart was toward them as they arrived.

My new house dad had been told about how strict my previous house dad had been. He thought he was supposed to keep discipline somewhat like him. Consequently, the paddle was used a lot in our home for discipline and control. He was in his mid-twenties when he became my dad—along with being dad to fourteen other kids. Most of the teenagers in our home were juvenile delinquents. They had been in trouble one way or another and had ended up at the home for rehabilitation. I was exposed to all kinds of information and saw kids do things that took away any innocence I had left as a young girl. The kids knew when and where to go to hide in order to do whatever they wanted to do. We hardly ever told on each other; it was an atmosphere of the adults against kids. I sometimes was made to stand guard and warn the older kids if an adult was coming. There were times that the teenagers who had done drugs had seizures or flashbacks and would become uncontrollable. This kept me from ever delving into drugs as I had watched them suffer in this way.

The school leadership believed that work and punishment would keep the kids doing well. So fear of punishment was the basis for behavior modification. This, of course, is a lie that causes destruction and devastation in the heart of a child. We needed emotional bonding, love, laughter and play, and instructive training from working alongside parents. I also needed someone to figure out why I was not doing well in school. The real issues of childcare never seemed to be important.

My house dad did buy a horse for us and always made sure that I was able to ride her. I think he knew this meant a lot to me. This little act of kindness towards me caused me to feel special. The horse's name was Babe. I loved riding that horse. She was a gentle, short American Quarter horse. The horse gift endeared me to my house dad. God was working through him in giving this gift to me. I have a relationship with this house dad as an adult. I know that he had no idea of what I had gone through before I was given to him to parent.

My new house mom was younger than dad and had the responsibility of taking care of five teenage girls and one younger girl. Three new girls and three new boys moved into our home. New to me, anyway. I quickly had to adjust to a whole new family. It was usual for children to leave with no prior notice. We did not get to say goodbye. New children came, and we just accepted the new ones as brothers and sisters. We really had no other choice. House moms had the responsibility of keeping order and control over the girls, as well as the upkeep of the house and laundry. We girls were put in charge of doing the chores around the house, including washing with a wringer-washing machine and hanging all the clothes out on the line to dry. I never used an inside, powered dryer until I was sixteen.

If we performed the way they thought we should, they left us alone. If we messed up somehow, they would relate to us through punishment. I was very bitter and hard to get along with—and stubborn. I hated people who were in authority over me; I lumped them all into one pot, believing they were there just to make my life miserable. I loved to sew; this house mom saw this and tried to show me love by letting me sew. She and my dad bought me a sewing machine for my ninth grade graduation present. This was a most special gift to me. I began to sew all my dresses. Sewing gave me an outlet of self worth and creativity as a teenager. God worked through this mom and her gift. I now have a good relationship with this mom as an adult. We have shared our hearts with each other. She had no idea of what

I had experienced before living with her. The leadership of the children's home would not share anything of a child's past with the parents who came to take responsibility for that child.

In the seventh grade a new *angel* friend came to the school. The other children did not want to be friends with her, but I always felt sorry for the new kids, so I said hi to her—from then on we were best friends. She moved into the house next door. We walked to school together and sat by each other in classes. We played basketball and tetherball, swung on swings, and rode our bikes together. All of a sudden one summer day my friend did not show up at the dining hall for lunch. We always did our jobs together, and so I was so surprised when she was not there. After I finished my job, I walked out of the dining hall and saw her house parents, with their own children, get in a van and drive away. I did not see my friend until the next school year. I asked her where she had been. Her house dad had been having an inappropriate physical relationship with her; someone had caught them together and had told. She was sent

out to a farm to live with a small family. He and his family were sent away to another children's home. I was so in shock—she was my age. I was only in the eighth grade.

During my teenage years I became involved with a Bible Bowl team. We would study two books of the Bible and have contests of questions in a game format where we buzzed in if we knew the answer. Being involved with Bible Bowl provided an avenue that was a huge help to me as a teenager in this strange world. It gave me a love for the Bible and a desire to study and seek out the truth for myself, all of which later would help me seek God out in relationship for myself.

There also was a small little *angel* who came into my life with these new house parents. They had a little son who was not even a year old at the time. He brought a huge ray of sunlight into my heart. Where I could not respond to any adult, I could emotionally bond with this little baby boy. I carried him everywhere and took care of him as much as I could. He became my little brother.

I protected him from the other kids who were at times mean to him because he was a house parent's child. They believed they were getting back at the house parents by being mean to their son. God allowed this little boy to keep a part of my heart open to love. When my house parents left the children's home, they too went on "vacation" and came back without their son. I never got to tell him goodbye. I knew instantly that they were leaving. Bitterness from losing the one person

I could love closed my heart. I would not hug them to say goodbye the day they left. They wanted to take me with them, but they were told I could not go with them. They shared this with me when they left. It helped my heart to know this. Years later I would get re-acquainted with this couple while I was in college. They helped me each semester with a gift of money, which enabled me to have clothes for school.

A very nice older girl moved into our home, and she was an *angel* to me. She had grown up at the home since she was a little girl. She and I became close. She was gentle and good. I decided I wanted to be like her and not like the girls I thought were bad. We stayed together until she graduated from high school. She became a missionary, teaching children in another country. She taught me how to take care of myself as a girl, keeping clean, fixing my hair, and wearing makeup.

I despised one of my eighth grade teachers. He was a very bitter man. A guy friend of mine was laughing in class one day at a fly on the floor. This teacher heard him laughing, then wrapped duct tape around this kid's head and face from his chin all the way up to under his nose. The boy was hardly able to get his breath. The humiliation was horrible for all of us as we watched him suffer at this abuse. My heart became so angry at the abuse I witnessed on a weekly basis. It seemed to me that nobody cared about what was happening or took action against the abuse.

My Senior High School Years

I graduated from ninth grade, and that summer my seventh set of parents left. I was left in limbo for about a month—not knowing where I would end up moving. Nobody came to talk to me or explain what was going to happen to me. I just had to wait and see. What happened next put me in shock, and I then believed that God was sadistic and did not care about me or my life at all. The house dad who had left the home because of an inappropriate relationship with my best friend returned with his wife and family to become parents again. I was told that I would be moving into their house as one of their girls. I could not believe my ears! I remained silent about what my girlfriend had told me. I moved into their house wondering why God was allowing this craziness to go on in my life. Right away I knew that there was validity to the story. This dad was not allowed to have any contact with us girls. He took care of the boys, and mom took care of us girls.

Right after moving in, I was given the responsibility of cleaning all the kitchen cabinets and arranging all the kitchen items in the cabinets. My house mom appreciated how well I did and praised me. So I learned that if I performed well, I would get along great with this house mother.

I was fifteen years of age, going into my sophomore year of high school. I wanted to have the reputation of being good, and so I became a robot that performed the ways the leadership and house parents wanted me to. I wanted to be invisible, to fade into the everyday activities of life, and to not have to run into any trouble with people. Every once in a while, the anger would burst from me. One time during an anger burst, I accidentally smashed a body mirror in pieces. I had been upset at my house parents for taking one of the children with them on their vacation and leaving me behind. I felt this was wrong for them to single out one child to take yet leave the rest of us. My heart felt like they loved him more than me. I was simply responding from a very abandoned, rejected heart.

As I got older, I figured out I must be pretty; the guys were wanting to talk to me more frequently. My house dad would act really weird every time a guy talked to me. He would come tell me to go into the house and do a job. I did not dare challenge him, as I had seen how he had reacted to other kids who challenged him. If I hung out with a guy, it was only in friendship. If he decided to try to hold my hand or touch me in any way, I would freeze as though I was paralyzed. I would then abandon the friendship. I did not like any kind of touching. The inappropriate touching I had endured in my earlier childhood caused me to dislike any guy to show me affection through touch.

About six months after moving into this home, the house dad began to show me attention. When I would be working in the dining hall at my job, he would come up behind me and lean his whole body into the back of mine, pretending to show me something about my job. Our family would go swimming, and he would come up to stand behind me in the pool and touch me inappropriately. I would freeze in these situations, not saying a word. One night coming home from a basketball game, with four other men in the van, he told me to sit between the front two seats on a box to make room for the other men. In the dark of the van, he ran his hand up and down my leg all the way home; again I was paralyzed and unable to say a word to anyone.

I saw him many times touch other girls inappropriately. He did this during times and in ways that he thought no one could see what he was doing. I could not bring myself to tell my house mother. I did not have an emotional, connected relationship with her. I felt like she would not believe me, and that I would be blamed and moved into another house. Being moved was a huge traumatic thought to me. My heart was confused between wanting a father/daughter relationship and also needing and desiring attention.

God saw what was happening, and he sent a young couple to the home who would become my youth group leaders. This *angel* couple had both grown up at the home and gone off to Bible college. They were returning to work at the home. I was growing in my relationship as a Christian, realizing what right and wrong behavior was and wanting in my heart to do right. I decided that I no longer wanted this attention from my house dad. After I came to trust this couple, I went to them one evening when I was a junior in high school. I first begged them that what I was going to share with them could not be told to anyone. I wanted them to hold me accountable for not allowing this touching to continue. They promised me they would honor my request to say nothing. Telling them my secret enabled me to hold myself accountable to someone if I became weak and allowed him to touch me again. This gave me a strange power of strength to not let it happen. We all know now that we should have brought it out into the open because of how other girls may have been affected by him after I left the home.

In high school we went to a public school in town, and the majority of the kids were of a different race. Many of the teachers were also. My race was a minority in this school. The children's home would take us to school on our own bus. We all were known as The Home Kids; I hated arriving at school on that bus and being known as one of those kids. It humiliated me. I dreaded going to school each day; socially I had been crippled and was very inhibited. I joked a lot, to hide my inhibitions, so people thought I was happy and well. I loved to learn, but not in math or science. I enjoyed the home economics, typing, English, and vocational business classes. It wasn't until my senior year, that I started coming out of my shell academically and made all A's.

One history teacher humiliated kids in front of the class. One time he told the class that he knew where the Garden of the Eden was in the Middle East. I thought that was interesting and asked him why he didn't travel over there to find out for himself if it was still there. He assumed I was making fun of him. I wasn't, I just thought it would be interesting for him to go. He made me come to the front of the class and draw a circle on the bottom of the chalk board. He asked me if I wanted to stick my nose in the circle. I was totally shocked and humiliated. I humbly said no, and he let me go back to my seat after he threatened to paddle me. I never spoke another word in his class. I did have two *angel* teachers who helped me to realize I had abilities and the capability to learn. One of the teachers taught the typing class, and the other teacher taught my vocational business classes. They knew how to encourage the potential in me. They treated all of us students the same with no favoritism.

During high school at the home, we were woken up at five in the morning to do a chore in the house assigned to us. These chores were mostly either laundry or cleaning the bathroom, kitchen, and living room. We did this cleaning every morning before breakfast, along with having to be dressed for school. Breakfast was at seven, and then we went off to Bible classes before we got on the bus for school. After school, we had another chore before supper. Then homework, family devotions, and off to bed by nine in the evening. On the weekend we did get free time after we did a big chore that was assigned to us. Saturday afternoons was usually when I would have time to design and sew clothes for myself. My housemother would not allow us girls to shower in the morning during the school week. My hair was only manageable if I washed it in the morning, so I would often ask to get the chore of cleaning the bathroom or doing laundry. This would enable me to be around water in order to secretly wash my hair in the process of doing my chore. I would then quickly run into my bedroom and dry my hair, hoping she would not catch me. We girls were required to wear dresses four days out of the week to school. Nobody else was wearing dresses to high school in the mid-seventies.

Blue jeans were in fashion. The humiliation of having to wear dresses lowered my self-esteem.

I needed a person to be able to talk over things with at this age. I would have liked to have been able to have time sharing and talking with my house mother about what was in my heart. But she had four little ones to care for, and as a house mom, her job was mostly a disciplinarian: keeping us all in order and making sure our chores were finished in the right way. It seemed like it was all about keeping us in good behavior and not about relationship at all. I never received the mothering and fathering that a child needed. It greatly affected how I mothered my own daughters, because I thought mothering was all about keeping order and discipline. I did not understand the heart-relationship aspect of loving. Looking back, this mom taught me how to perform in all the right ways to look like a godly woman. She stood up for me at times when others would try to come against me. She taught me how to keep a clean and neat home. I wish she could have ministered to my heart in a relationship. I believe that the most important reason God calls people to minister at a children's home is to minister to the children's hearts.

The Bible Bowl was my avenue for sanity and freedom. I was able to go on trips away from the children's home. We traveled to other churches to play games with other teams. I saw that there was another world out there and knew that someday I would be a part of that world. God gave me an awesome Bible Bowl teacher. She became one of my *angels*. She was an older woman who came alongside me as an encourager. Throughout my high school years she hired me to do odd jobs for her, so that I could earn my own money. This money helped me to have something that was my own. With the money I earned working for her, I was able to buy a nice bicycle. This bicycle came in handy with getting to my summer job at the food warehouse at the home. Also, it became my vehicle for getting around during my first year of college.

As my graduation from high school drew near, I knew that I would be allowed to finally meet my real birth mother. She and my father had put us four girls up for adoption, and we had become wards of the state. We could not see either of them by court order until we graduated from high school. My parents had divorced, my mom remarried, and my father was traveling with the carnival across the country. All my life I had dreamed of meeting my mother. What was she like? What would I say to her? Would she like me? Was she pretty? Would she run to me and hug me? It was all surreal.

The day finally came for us to meet. I was to graduate the next day, and my house mom picked me up from my last day at school. I got out of our vehicle and walked up the stairs into our house. There sitting on the couch was my real, live birth mother. She just sat there looking at me. I just stood there looking at her. Finally, I walked over to her and reaching down to where she was sitting, I put my arms around her and gave her a hug. She began to cry. I did not know what to say, so I said, "I love you, mom." I felt no emotion at all. This woman was a stranger to me. I was doing what I thought I should do in the situation. My oldest sister was there also with my mother's husband. My sister introduced me to my step-dad. He was pretty cool, and he had a hot rod they had driven down in to see me graduate from high school. He let me drive his car the whole weekend they were visiting. We went to stay together at a hotel for the next couple of days. That night I graduated from high school, and my mother was there and watched me graduate. It had been a long wait on her part to see her daughter again. I cannot imagine the pain she experienced in her life having to give up four little girls.

I later learned that my mother at the age of twelve found her own father hanging by the neck in their garage. I am told he had cancer at the time. My mother also had two sisters. The devastation to their family because of this tragedy was huge. I believe my mother never recovered from her father's death. She was the oldest daughter and loved her father dearly. At this time in my life, I did make a conscious choice to not return home with my mother. I wanted a different life and knew that I could not have it if I went to live with her. This proved out to be a God-directed decision.

Stepping Out on My Own

In the fall of 1977, I chose to go to a nearby Bible college. I had attended a high school retreat at that college my senior year. One afternoon, while standing out on the deck of a dormitory at the college, I felt this presence of serenity around me. In my mind, I suddenly knew that I was to go to school here, and that my future would be directed through this avenue. I believe it was heavenly guidance from God. He promises in the Bible to be a Father to the fatherless (Psalm 68:5). He was guiding His daughter's next step. Although, I was fearful of moving too far away from what I knew, my youth group leaders had attended this same college—so I decided to follow in their tracks. I was given a job on campus in the cafeteria to help pay for my schooling. I became a good student and made good grades. I enjoyed studying the Bible courses.

Several months after starting college, I went to visit my real mom and step-dad in their hometown. While there, I thought I would stop by and visit the set of foster parents I had lived with prior to moving to the children's home. A strange intervention happened. Two days before I arrived to visit, the foster dad passed away. The whole family was attending the funeral on the day I arrived, and I had to be back at school the following day. I did not get to see my foster mother. Two years later I went back again, planning on seeing her. The day I arrived she died suddenly. In my heart I heard clearly a voice of guidance saying to me, "I rescued you from this place and atmosphere, do not return. Continue on the path I have shown you." I again felt this was God speaking guidance to me. So I continued my education and worked in the summers taking care of elderly people and at a private day care.

My sophomore year of college, several guys began to ask me out on dates. I would go occasionally, but no one really captured my attention. If I felt like they were not the one for me, I chose not to go out with them again. I enjoyed learning and was focusing on my studies. One day, I began to take notice of a particular young man. He was always hanging out before a class of mine where he had a class in the next room over. He seemed very nice to everyone he talked with. He joked with me once, but it seemed like it was just in passing, so I figured he wasn't too interested in me. One night I decided I would go with a team to visit older people in a nursing home. As we were driving home, the guy who was driving our car pulled over to talk with a guy driving the other car. I noticed that the other driver was this young man. I listened as they visited, and he looked at me in the eye a couple of times and smiled. I smiled back, and the driver of my car introduced us.

A few days later he was in my classroom when I got there. As I came in, he got up to leave and said hello to me. I smiled and said hello back. He kept showing up every day in my classroom, and finally, I got a phone call from him. He asked me if I would go with him to a movie. I had a babysitting job for a family and could not pass up the money if they needed me for that evening. So I told him I did not know, but would call him back. His buddies were waiting in his dorm room to see what my answer had been. He had to go back to his room and tell them that I had said, "I do not know." I felt so bad for him when he told me about this later.

The next day, I called him and accepted. I already knew his name was Dan. Everyone I talked to about him told me that he was the most awesome person on campus. They also told me that he had never taken a girl out on a second date before. Well, we went to the movies, got some pizza, and walked through an animal-petting zoo all on our first date. I immediately was comfortable with this guy. We became great friends and loved being together.

I guess he liked me also; we did go on that second date, and after two months of knowing him, I decided not to date anyone else. He was very kind and considerate—not just of me, but I saw how he treated everyone with the same kind of consideration. When he talked with someone, it seemed as though that person was the only person in the world. I also noticed that he even talked with people I believed to be weird, and he gave them the same time and consideration in listening to them. A married couple on campus knew my house parents, and they phoned and told them that I was dating the nicest guy on campus. As the end of the year and Dan's graduation neared, he asked me if I would marry him and become his wife. We planned a May wedding after I would graduate the next year, but by the next fall, Dan decided he wanted to get married in January and prepare to move to the state of Alaska the next June. So, in the beginning of 1980, we married, worked for six months to save money, and took off together for a life of adventure to Alaska.

I was ready and willing for an adventure; I felt free for the first time in my life. I believed that Dan and I would move to Alaska and be involved in a church ministry together. He had done a ministry internship for a summer in Alaska. We had both attended Bible college, and so I thought he would look for a job in a church setting. His first job he got in Alaska was cleaning fish at a cannery for five dollars an hour. Two weeks after arriving in Alaska, he was called and offered a ministry position in the state of Tennessee, and I wanted to go. He turned the job down, and I was devastated with this new husband of mine. We borrowed money to purchase a used trailer home, and we moved into our new home in Alaska. I found a job at a childcare center near the trailer home. Dan eventually took a job at a mail express company.

He worked three days, then would go hunting or fishing for three days. On Sundays, we attended church together. I soon grew tired of this lifestyle. I did not realize that Dan was out to prove to himself that he was a man through conquering the Wild Frontier. Dan grew up being the youngest child in his family. Being the youngest put him in a position of having to follow everyone else and not being allowed to make his own decisions for himself. In becoming a man on his own, he began a journey of proving that he *was* a real man, fully able to make decisions on his own, not having to depend upon others for advice or direction.

The church we attended was where Dan had completed his summer college internship the summer before we got married. Everyone there knew Dan. I didn't feel accepted in this church, and I expressed that to Dan. He listened to my feelings, but never took any action in finding another church. In this church, I felt like I was not living up to their expectations of what a Christian woman was to be. I wanted to build relationships, but no one was interested in coming into a friendship or allowing me to become a part of their lives. I felt like I was expected to perform a certain way and that I was not acceptable unless I could. Church was all about growing and performing in that growth. I had to achieve a certain standard in order to become acceptable to them and to God. Everybody had their own ideas about the way God wanted us to perform.

It seemed as though there was an inside group in this church who supposedly had achieved this standard of growth. Then there was the second level of people who weren't quite living up to the standard that had been set. Then there were those who knew they could never live up to the standard, so why try? These people didn't stay at church very long before they left. The church was not about getting to know the hearts of people and walking in a relationship with them. I tried to just push down my feelings and be a good Christian wife. I now know that God was speaking through me to my husband about relationship, using how I felt to communicate to Dan. He designed for us to be heirs together of the grace of life in our marriage (I Peter 3:7b).

A couple of women came to tell me things I was doing wrong. They never could explain why they were wrong. One of the women was a minister's wife from another town. She told me that I was wild. I did not know how my behavior was wild; she never offered that information. I assumed that because she was a minister's wife, she knew what she was talking about, so I tried to calm down and perform meekly and quietly. Just like at the children's home—if I stayed quiet and out of the way, everyone thought I was a wonderful, Christian woman. I was not being the unique person God had created me to be. The performance-driven religious society was not allowing me to walk in the freedom of the New Covenant. I know now that God desired His people to love and befriend me unconditionally. To come alongside me and get to know who I was in a relationship. To find out about my childhood and lead me to healing for my heart and soul. Church is to be a community of believers relating to and helping each other out. Dan and I did not know about heart relationships with God. We knew of God, but we had never been taught about walking in an intimate, emotionally-connected relationship with God in our everyday lives.

Alaska was very scary for me. I was afraid of the city life in Anchorage. I was afraid to even walk down a city street. I was internally afraid of everyone and every new thing. I had been sheltered in the children's home and was now living in a world I did not understand. I remember I was terrified of the ocean. To go fishing we would drive along a highway right next to the Pacific Ocean. I was terrified that our car would veer off into the ocean and we would drown. Dan did not realize the amount of fear and trauma I had lived through. He did not know how terrified this young wife of his was of the world where he had brought her to live. He was out to conquer the world, and I was terrified of this same world. Consequently, I was always trying to protect myself, and he was always walking on the dangerous side of life. I believed that being a good Christian wife meant that Dan was always to make the decisions as the head of our home and that he was right. I was supposed to submit, go along with everything he wanted, and let my own needs and desires be pressed down. This is how I had seen my house moms relate to their husbands. I remained quiet about the church, and I suffered there emotionally and spiritually. I allowed him to hunt and fish as much as he wanted. He did not walk in a relationship with God. But Dan was pleasant, good, and kind and went to church, so he looked like a godly, Christian man. Dan knew about God, but he did not walk with God in a relationship. I began to inwardly develop bitterness at Dan due to him not caring for me emotionally.

He did not realize we needed to be in a relationship of working things out *together* as coheirs of the grace of God.

Three and a half years into our marriage, I became pregnant with our first daughter. Dan and I had never decided to have children. We let it happen naturally. He came home from a hunting trip and I ran out to the car, excited to tell him that I was pregnant. When I told him, I expected him to pick me up in his arms, twirl me around, and be excited. He was unloading the back of his car; he looked at me, shut the trunk of the car, and turned to walk into our home. I followed after him, looking for some kind of acknowledgment of what I had shared. Emotionally, he did not respond to the news. He began to ask me how I knew I was pregnant. Inwardly he was interested. He just could not feel emotionally about things. I did not know it at the time, but as a young man, he was emotionally shut down and therefore could not feel emotions. Dan was always on an even keel, and people saw that as godliness. They did not realize his heart had been wounded.

Dan came to all the Lamaze classes with me during my pregnancy. He was right there for the birth of every one of our three daughters. He provided well for us. He just could not emotionally care for us. He believed I could take care of myself. I did not know how due to the fact that I was still a little girl trying to live in a woman's body and live a woman's life in a woman's world. My *angels* during this time were two women. First was a friend who was the mother of six children. When I became pregnant with my first child, she befriended me and took me to breast-nursing classes. Here I learned how to nurse and care for my baby. Second was a woman who came alongside me as a substitute mother figure. She was there for me whenever I needed mothering. She would fix meals when I was sick. She would let me share with her my heart. She gave me my first baby shower. She babysat my daughters so I could go on a trip with my husband. She opened her heart and her home to me and my family. My daughters still call her grandma. These two *angels* showed me that love really was about giving and serving others through relationship. These two women were true Christians who allowed Jesus to live through them in loving me.

Turning My Life Over

One afternoon, when my first daughter was two years old, I put her down for a nap. The day before I had received a package in the mail from one of my house moms. In it was a book entitled *The Christian's Secret to A Happy Life,* by Hannah Whithall Smith. I went to sit on my bed and began to read this book. In the middle of the second chapter, I put down the book, lay on my bed, and began to cry out to God. My life was miserable, and I knew the Christian life I was living was not a happy one. I turned my unhappy life over to God and asked Him to make my life what He wanted it to be. My spirit was filled with peace, and I knew something significant had happened. God accepted my offer and took over the responsibility for my life. I began to communicate with Him about everything in my life. I began to have an understanding of what was wrong and right in my heart. I no longer desired in my heart to do the wrong. I no longer was fearful about my life. He was the authority I chose to place myself under, and I was making this choice out of my own free will. I was not being forced.

At this point, though, my picture of God was still misconstrued by the authority of abuse I had lived under as a child. I did not know how good and loving God was; I still believed Him to be a God who punished. I was obeying Him with a motivation of being blessed—and to look godly. I wanted to be godly, so others would see me and call me a godly woman. I had been raised to believe this was a woman's priority and identity. I still wanted to measure up to people's godly standards, become acceptable to them, and be an insider. I had no idea that I was a unique person and that God loved who I was and accepted me. He knew me completely—with all my abusive past and wrong motivations and concepts. He knew what I needed and would make provision for everything in my life. He was delighted that I had chosen to come to Him. I began to walk in the light of His presence, and the darkness and some of the fears went away. I was able to express myself easier around people. As I continued to read through the book, I began to realize and understand that sometimes people who talk and act like they know everything are not always right.

I began to question everything I had been taught about God and living the Christian life. I had always done what I was told to do out of fear. God had to break that mold and bondage. It was dangerous to break that mold, but God wanted me out of a motivation of love, not fear. Legalistic people are afraid of people who are breaking out of their molds and begin to question theologies and traditions. I no longer tried to fit the mold. Then I really didn't fit in at church anymore. I was considered rebellious. Jesus didn't quite fit into the synagogue scene either. The leadership in His day wanted to find a way to silence Him. God finally was able to help me see that it was Jesus who set the standard for me. He enabled me to be an insider. Inside God's family, acceptable to God as His daughter. He desired to come along beside me in relationship and show me what His love was all about. Before God could get me to this place, He had to let me fail again and again, until I lost all my own strength. The following is an analogy that God showed me one day of when He rescued me.

Slave Market Day

It is slave market day. The slaves are dragged out by their chains and left to the scrutiny of the buyers. The price bidding begins and slaves are selling right and left. There are those slaves who have great strength. There are some who have pride in themselves, still able to hold their chins and shoulders straight. Others are young and have many years left for service to work for a master. These are the ones who are quickly chosen by the slave owners. Finally, all eyes fell on the final slave on the block. There came a gasp and then laughter quickly followed as the bidder asks for a bid. Small, weak, worn out, no pride left in her, utterly surrendered to the condition of worthlessness and helplessness, who would want such a one as I? A bid that is least required by law was yelled out of the crowd of slave owners. Laughter again. No life is left within me to care who is buying me this time. All has been drained from me by my bondage to other slave owners. Then it happened. Out of the crowd came a gentle, kind voice that said with authority, "I choose this one to be mine. I will pay the highest price for this one." Many in the crowd mocked the price that is paid for me. They leave the block in disgust that such a price would be paid for me. I understand their mocking and disgust, for I am broken in every sense of the word. What use could this master want me for? Then I heard my new master's voice again, only He is speaking right beside me. I watched as the slave trader hands over the keys to my chains, and as my new master takes the keys and unlocks them. He withdraws the chains from around me, places a light garment around me, and lifts me to my feet. He, says, "Arise, my child, lean on me and let us go away from this place. Let us go home." I am bewildered, all my years as a slave is causing me total confusion and unbelief. I do not dare trust this gentleness and kindness coming from the voice of my new master. Am I dreaming? Have I been deceived? Is this really the truth or have I gone crazy? Did he call me his child? Am I to walk beside Him? He brings me to his house. He begins to serve me. He gives me milk to drink, for in my weakened state I cannot eat meat. As I become strengthened day by day, he begins to feed me bread. All my needs are provided. Each day, He talks with me. He tells me I am no longer a slave to my former master. That my old way of life is over. I am to be his child. He has legally made me his daughter. I am to share and inherit all that is His.

I can not comprehend all that has now become mine. In my former life, I worked hard until I had no strength left. I served masters who could not be satisfied. They wanted perfection. I did all I could to please my old masters, but I never accomplished that goal. They could never be satisfied. My work would always be lacking and then end in failure in some way. I would go to my former masters and listen closely to their words of what to do and how to do it. I would spend days preparing. I had all the knowledge, but something was lacking, for in the end I would fail. One day when I was walking and talking in the garden with my Father, that's right, for I have truly become His child, not a slave, He is listening to me. I tell Him of my former life, and I ask Him what it was that I lacked. As I listen, He speaks to me of love. My heart is overwhelmed with His words to me. I begin to understand the high price he has paid for my life. As He loves me, I become renewed day by day. My wounds are being cleansed and healing begins taking place in the restoration of my soul. My life is so full of His love. One day, I ask Him, "How can I repay you for this love?"

He replies, "I have loved you freely. My love is a gift. You cannot repay me."

I cry out, "But my heart is so full of your love, I want to do something to show you how much I love you."

My father takes me by the hand, looks into my eyes, and speaks these words to me. "Having you here, you being free from slavery, you gaining strength and healing, you laughing and living in peace and contentment. Our being in a relationship, you knowing that I love you and will never leave you or send you away, this is all I have ever desired for you. This is my payment." Months go by and my healing continues.

One morning, my Father comes to me and says, "I am going to the slave market again today. I would like for you to go with me." At first, I am fearful to return to that place of memory. But this day, I am going not as a slave, but as a child of a free person. I watch as my Father sets another slave free, and together we bring this child to our home. I help my Father as He cares every day for this weak child. We, together, give the milk and then bread and on to meat. As my Father has loved me, so now I am loving this child in the same manner. After this day, I come to better understand how great my Father is, and I see how this inheritance of freedom I have been given is unending. The supply for my needs and others' needs will never run dry. I know that there are still many left in bondage that my Father longs to see set free. In my heart, I also am now longing for these to be set free. For others to know and have this relationship of freedom and love. Where once I was a slave, in bondage and fear, I now am free with a heart that loves. My inheritance will enable me to bring freedom and love into the slave market and bring others home to my Father's house.

As I began to walk with God, He began to show me that whenever I spoke to Dan about concerns I had, I should wait on the right timing. He also showed me that it was He who would convince Dan to listen to me and take action. One day I shared with Dan that I wanted to move out of the city and go to the country. I would be more at peace in the country, because of how the city frightened me. I could not envision raising our children in the city. Two weeks after I shared this with Dan, our newspaper had a picture of a very nice home out in the country. It was half the price of what a home in the city would cost us to buy. Our state at the same time came out with a program to help first time home buyers get into homes. Dan started to consider the country move. We decided to go look, and after finding three homes we could easily get into, we put in a bid for two of the homes, and won one of the bids. We sold our trailer and moved the beginning of that summer. In my heart, I knew that God had arranged all this for us, and when I walked with Him, life was easier; and I was able to rest.

Soon after moving, I gave birth to our third daughter. Our oldest daughter was starting kindergarten. I was living the life I had always dreamed of living. I was a wife, a mother of three beautiful daughters, and we were living in the country and breathing the fresh mountain air. But something was missing in my relationship with Dan. As I walked with God, I wanted Dan to join in on that walk. Whenever we had to make a decision, I would want to ask God. This offended him, because in his heart, he felt like the youngest in the family again, having to follow someone else's lead. His heart had been wounded, during his life by nobody asking him for his advice, direction, or thoughts. He always felt he had to follow. Now as an adult he wanted to be the leader. He wanted to be in control over the direction his family would go. By golly, he was the man and he was going to decide! He believed himself to be godly because he was good and was keeping all the standards that had been set up before him as a child.

He did not know that walking with and knowing God in relationship was why Jesus had saved him. It was too painful for his wounded heart to let God be in charge. He believed in his heart that God would try to run his life and decide what was best for him all the time, and not let Dan in on the decisions about his own life. He did not want a God who would run his life. He wanted to show himself and the world that he was capable of being the leader and making decisions all on his own. To come to God would be substantiating all the lies he had believed about himself when he was young.

I understood out of my own relationship with God, that Dan did not walk with God in an intimate way. I did not know then, that God was going to pursue and reach Dan through my own broken heart. We were going to go through the valley of the shadow of death. But God would bring us to the other side into what God calls abundant life. I resented Dan's rejection of my walk with God. He was making me feel again the wounds of my heart. Wounds of making me obey him out of force, with no choice on my part in the decision. He was robbing me of my newfound freedom and life. If I disagreed with his decisions, he would respond by abandoning me and going hunting, fishing, or working on a project. He could not emotionally care for me.

My heart needed Dan's emotional caring in order to heal. His heart needed me to believe in him and his decisions. God desired to get my performance-based motivation to come to an end. He also wanted me to see the damage and infection that were festering inside my heart. God desired to cause Dan's outward, good-looking life to come to an end. He wanted Dan to realize that without His loving guidance,

Dan could not succeed in this fallen world. God wanted to bring leading and guidance that would not force Dan to follow, but come alongside Dan's own heart's desires to be a man and make wise decisions.

I was not content and felt trapped in my marriage to Dan. I was feeling controlled and stifled, and that I was missing out on life. After my two older girls were in school, I applied for a job and was hired as a cashier. I was very successful at my job, because I gave it my all. I never did anything half-hearted. If I couldn't give my all, I didn't think it was worth my effort. After a while the job lost its appeal, and I wondered what was wrong with me. At this point Dan and I did not know how to emotionally care for one another. We went through a crisis at this point in our marriage, and it was during this time, that we both made a decision to love each other as best we knew how. This was a turning point for me, as I now was choosing to focus on living for Dan as a one-man woman. This is when I really began to care for Dan and desire to be one with him emotionally and spiritually.

I cried out to God and asked Him, "What should I do?" The next day a lady came up to my cashier counter to check out what she was purchasing. She handed me a check to pay for her items. A verse of scripture on her check said, "For where your treasure is, there will your heart, be also" (Matthew 6:21). All of a sudden I knew God was wanting me to see that verse. I looked at the lady quickly, hoping she couldn't see that I was startled. I helped her with her purchase and she was gone. I leaned back on the stand behind me, and a question popped into my mind. "What is your treasure?" God was asking me what was my treasure.

"Well, my treasure is my girls, Dan, and of course my relationship with You." I didn't realize at the time that God was third on my list and that my girls and Dan were placed before Him. What I did consider was that my heart was wanting to be with my daughters and Dan, pouring into their lives my energy and love. In less than a month, I resigned my job and went back home. I now put all into my family. The reality was that my girls came first, Dan next, and then God. I didn't know it then, but God was desiring to heal my heart in relationship to Him. He knew that my heart was so damaged I could not trust my girls and my husband to His care. I was still living with a wrong concept of whom He was, and so I was still performing out of fear to get His blessing and not receive His judgement.

Legalism & God's Ordained Collapse

I laid down all in order to give all to my treasure. My treasure was where my heart was hiding. I believed if I could be an awesome mother to my daughters and raise them correctly, then I would have my heart's desire. There was a hitch to my plans, though. I had been taught wrongly what being a mother was all about. I believed it was about putting the right stuff in and keeping out all the wrong stuff. I thought I could best raise my daughters with sheltering and discipline. I had no idea that it was a heart relationship I needed to keep my daughters' hearts from desiring the wrong paths.

The first step I made was to bring my girls home from public school and home school them. My girls were young enough, so they did not put up any argument about coming home for school. I proceeded to keep them busy with school and chores. They also were able to do many adventure trips with Dan and myself. I was with my girls, but as they got older, the things we would not let them participate in caused their hearts to harden towards us. I had no idea how to fellowship with their hearts in relationship. I did not realize that my heart had never been taught relationship. I had only been taught what you should or should not do in life. Those things were always changing based on who you talked with or were in relationship with. I began to walk in legalism, believing if I kept all the right ways of God, He would bless my family. Legalism was a place of safety and security for me. I walked in fear of failure, rejection, and punishment. "There is no fear in love, but perfect love casts out fear: Because fear has torment. He that fears is not made perfect in love" (I John 4:18).

The next fall, Dan and I went to a conference in Anchorage for home-school families. The speakers were a family who had begun to home church their family and move away from what they called the worldly ways. Looking back, I should have waited on God and Dan to lead us. Instead of consulting God, my bondage to doing everything right took over and I began to lead our family in this direction. We began to wear dresses only, stopped watching television, and stopped going to movies. We tried to follow the guidelines this family had set for their family in walking in "godly" ways. It no longer was our walk with God, but trying to perform and become "holy" so that God would bless us as a family. God allowed me, because His plan for me was complete failure, so that my heart would realize my need for Him and grace. I was still in the treadmill of accomplishing my dreams, goals, and my Christianity. My independent righteous life needed to come to an end. This is what began a long journey to failure, despair, and a final blow to my already damaged heart.

My confusion as a Christian, mother, and wife was huge. I was torn between living by the law and walking by grace, but did not realize it at the time. My husband's nonrelationship with God was confusing me. I was bewildered with what directions we should go as a family. Once again, we decided to put the girls back into public school. Feeling unneeded at home, I went back to work. Our oldest daughter was pulling away from us, and I was desperate to hang onto her. Our middle daughter was getting obscene calls from young boys at school. Our youngest daughter, who was in kindergarten, was getting picked on at school from a young boy who was saying pornographic things to her and touching her every day at school. She would come home from school crying. I panicked and immediately wanted to bring the girls home again to school. Dan decided to wait until Christmas break in hopes that I would change my mind. I was so paralyzed by fear I would not reconsider. When we brought them home, one of our daughters did not want to come at all and was very angry about our decision. We were at a loss as to what else to do. We decided to go to a spiritual warfare counselor we had heard at a conference. We spent a lot of money to go, but nothing was resolved. We tried to put her in a rehabilitative home. We spent lots of money going there for an interview, and we were told it was going to work out. But we never heard back from them. Later we found out that they were going through administrative changes and just dropped the ball with us. We did not realize it, but we were going in the opposite direction than we should have been going with our daughter. We were driving her farther away, and we were at a loss as how to regain her heart. Struggles had also begun with our relationship with one of our other daughters.

At this point I was exhausted of all my strength—physically, spiritually, and emotionally. I had cried, prayed, fasted, memorized Scripture, and been to many conferences to try to get help. I could not read the Bible either, because whenever I stood on a truth, it never became a reality for me. I was placing truth over the pain in my heart. Truth can never penetrate a heart that is wounded. Wounding in a heart must be healed by the Spirit of God; only then truth can enter the heart. Truth thrown at a wound only causes more pain to a person's heart. Just like a wound in the leg, if you do not clean it before you wrap it, infection will set in and the leg will get worse not better. I would be sitting in church during worship and just begin to sob, and I could not stop. Of course, this totally embarrassed Dan and the church people. He either wanted to leave or have me stop the crying. God was in the beginning processes of healing my heart, and a lot of infection was coming up. To stop my heart from crying would have been like trying to stop a volcano from erupting in mid air. All the desires of my heart had been destroyed, and I had nothing left to dream of or have vision for in my life. My treasure was being destroyed and my heart also in the process. I was in the process of failing in the very area where I wanted success. God kept me here in order to do intense surgery on my heart, so that I would come to know the magnitude of His grace and unconditional love.

During this time, we were offered an early out from Dan's job and a ministry in another state had offered Dan and me a position. So we put our home up for sale, took the early out, and waited for our move to take place. The ministry was to call us with the details of our move, but weeks went by without them calling. One morning Dan and I sat down on our bed and asked God to let us hear from the ministry. We asked for Him to show us His will in the phone call for whatever He wanted to happen in our lives. In two hours we had a phone call from the ministry saying that the board had decided that they did not have the funds to hire us for that position. They did not make an offer for another position. Wow, we then knew this was God's leading. Miraculously, Dan got his job back. However, the house had already sold, so we rented a house farther out of town.

We began to home church and continued to home school our daughters. We had a wonderful winter as a family, snowmobiling on seven acres of land and just being together. After a winter of this, we all felt like we needed and wanted fellowship with other Christians. So we started visiting churches in our community. We began to search out the theology that we had been taught growing up about God. We decided to visit different churches and see what other denominations were teaching. We were searching for truth, ourselves, and a foundation on which we could base our belief system. We found a church and began to fellow-ship there. Right after this, the house we were renting sold, and we moved closer into town.

One day, during this struggle, I was reading in the Bible where John the Baptist told the crowd that when Jesus came, He would give them the Holy Spirit to empower them and bring them into relationship with the Father in Heaven. As I meditated on that portion of Scripture, I realized that John was talking about believers like me that needed God's fellowship, peace, counsel, direction, and guidance. I went out on my front porch, looked up to heaven, and said out loud,

"Jesus, John said you would send and give to me the Holy Spirit and empower me with the ministry of the Holy Spirit, so I give you permission to allow the Holy Spirit to come to me and to work in and through me as you so desire. I want the Holy Spirit to bring me into a closer relationship with God."

I had never heard much spoken or taught about the Holy Spirit. During the next week, I came upon a poster about a conference in the city on none other than the Holy Spirit. I was so excited! I signed up and went. At this conference, I learned that the Holy Spirit indwells us in order to help us communicate with God and to guide and encourage us as children of God. I wondered why I had never heard this kind of teaching before in the churches I had attended my whole life. I soon found out that there are many controversies and fears about the Holy Spirit. From this period on, in my life communication with God became a whole new relationship. The Scriptures came alive to me. I knew without a doubt that God is alive and present within me. Here are some of the descriptions and passages in the Bible that tell about the Holy Spirit:

1. He is the Spirit of the Living God (II Corinthians 3:3b).

2. He is the Spirit of Truth that dwells in us (John 14:17).

3. He helps us talk to God and helps us know what God is saying to us (Romans 8:26 and Ephesians 2:18).

4. He lets us know when we have been wrong or have committed sin (John 16:8).

5. He comforts, protects, and guides us into all truth (John 14:26, 16:13 and Romans 8:14).

6. He reveals wisdom and revelation to us about Jesus in the Holy Bible (Ephesians 1:17).

7. He shows us things that are going to happen in the future (John 16:13).

8. He gives us special gifts so that we may help and love others (I Corinthians 12:8–31).

9. He produces or grows in us the Fruit of; Love, Joy, Peace, Patience, Kindness, Goodness, Gentleness, Faithfulness, and Self Control (Galatians 5:22).

10. He changes us into the likeness of Jesus Christ (II Corinthians 3:17).

An awesome *angel* couple came into my life at this time. They had a counseling ministry in the community where we lived. They helped me move out of a fearful and performance-based relationship with God into a loving and grace-filled walk with God. This woman and her husband loved me unconditionally and walked with me in a grace-filled relationship. The Holy Spirit worked through them for several years to minister to me God's story of grace and love. Their relationships with me were the bridge God used to help me cross over into the truth of who is God and that He loves and wants to be in relationship with me.

A course on living under the New Covenant came into my life through this *angel* couple. God began to show me how messed up my belief system was about Him. He began to reveal that I was His daughter and that His love for me was unconditional. He showed me that I believed Him to be a judgmental and punishing God. He showed me that under the law of good and evil, which is the Old Covenant, sin had to be punished. But His justice and wrath had been poured out onto Jesus on the cross, which made Jesus become sin for us. Therefore, we now live under grace, which is the New Covenant of eternal life. Justice for our sins has been paid, and the law was fulfilled by Jesus for everyone. Under the New Covenant, God guides me from within by His writing on my heart and mind His laws, and He lives through me by the indwelling of His Holy Spirit. More about this New Covenant can be read about in Hebrews 8–10 in the Bible.

This brought me into a relationship with a loving Father. A loving Father to come alongside me and guide me into all truth about this new relationship with Him. This relationship would be based on our relationship as Father and daughter, not based on my performance. This covenant allowed me to be changed into the likeness of Jesus Christ. I could come to Him without fear of punishment or judgment. He would walk gently with me. God's motivation was for me to be in a relationship of love and understanding. I could approach Him about any issue in my life. God began to show me how damaged and wounded my soul was and that He wanted to restore my soul. My soul consisted of my mind, my will, and my emotions.

Because of the fear and trauma I had lived under as a child, I was afraid of life. I felt alone in a gigantic world of peril. He showed me that He was always within me—I was not alone. He was for me and not against me. He revealed to me that He was bigger, more powerful, and had over-come the perils that were in the world. I began to walk in this new relationship with a God who was peaceful, under-standing, and restorative. God began to heal and restore the little girl that had been so damaged. It was at this moment that I wrote "Slave Market Day." The picture in this story was the understanding that God was giving my heart of the bondage I had been in and how He rescued me from that slavery, bringing me to the relationship He wanted with me. Through bringing me into this grace and unconditional love relationship with Him, God was revealing to me how He wanted me to come into relationship with my husband, my daughters, and others. I was now on a new path that led out of the hell I had been living through and into a heaven I had not known before.

RESTORATION OF MY HEART

Visiting friends one summer brought Dan and I into connection with a video of a marriage counselor who taught about the emotional connection that was needed in relationships. He shared why this connection does not happen and how it could begin to happen in our relationships. I was so interested in hearing more, I ordered the tapes, twelve in all, and started watching them. Dan would see me watching them and walk by thinking, "There's Birdie watching another teaching video."

I knew these teachings held the answer to some of the issues we were dealing with in our relationship, so I kept watching. After two months, I called the counselor's office to arrange a time for us—as a couple—to meet with him. There was a waiting list of five years with couples trying to get in to see this counselor. I signed up, believing that God was able to move this mountain. Dan didn't mind; he figured it was so long a wait, it would not happen. We ended up only waiting three and a half years, but God did not waste those years. He began a healing process in my heart that prepared me for that one week in Colorado.

My real mother mailed me some baby pictures of myself. They looked so much like our third daughter that I could not tell who was who. Over the next few months, God would remind me of something abusive or traumatic that happened to me, and a question would be impressed upon my mind: "If this would happen to your youngest daughter at this age, how would you feel?" I would begin to weep and cry out in pain, realizing what had taken place to the little girl in whose body I was living. I suddenly understood that I had been through a lot of trauma and needed to be healed from that damage. God then began to show me that He wanted me to grieve all of the trauma from my childhood and be able to forgive all that had happened to me. I then remembered that Jesus had stated, "One needs to forgive from the heart" (Matthew 18:35).

One afternoon, I was in a Bible bookstore and saw a picture of a little girl sitting on a white swing on a large porch. She was looking down at a big teddy bear that had fallen off the swing. Under the picture were these words, "Tho your mother and father forsake you, I will never leave you, nor will I forsake you." I just stood there and began to cry. The little girl reminded me of the woman on the swing who had tried to give me the teddy bear so that another woman could leave me. I knew God was speaking His healing words into my heart. I was able to begin to see and believe that God was for me and not against me and that I could trust Him with my life. I cried a lot those days, and Dan did not understand nor know how to handle my emotional breakdown. I describe it now like when a person decides to clean out the garage after many years of filling it with stuff. They get to the middle of the job and are surrounded with garbage piles and just a few items of any worth or value. They wonder why they ever decided to do this in the first place. They realize the only way out is to keep on going forward. Two books that helped me through this process were: Lifetime Guarantee by Bill Gilliam and Silent Killers of the Faith by Steve Crosby. I have read these two books at least four times each; they helped me think rightly about my relationship with God. They helped continue to get the truth inside my heart so that I would walk through truth. They were like an antibiotic—the truths written in these books entered my soul and killed all the lies I had believed and based my life upon. I began to walk in grace for my own life, my husband's, and my daughters' lives.

We finally got the call to come to Colorado for our week with the counselor. Dan started to drag his heels, but I remained steadfast about going. My reason was that I knew Dan did not show any emotion or walk in an intimate relationship with God. I was wanting to go so that Dan could get help. One of the testimonies on the teaching tape was of a minister of thirty years whose heart had been locked for most of his life. I believed that Dan was spiritually and emotionally locked up in his heart. I did not know why or how. I truly believed this counselor could help Dan get free. I already understood that I needed help also, but God used the desire in my heart toward my husband to compel me onward.

So we flew to Colorado a month later. We had no idea that Jesus was going to meet us there in a powerful encounter with Himself, not just in a meeting with the counselor. From the point of walking into the office, a pain welled up in my heart that was so fierce, I ran from the office to my car. After lunch, we went again to the office and as I turned to greet the counselor, my heart became overwhelmed with pain again. I began to cry and sob like a little baby. In a calming voice the counselor began to talk with us. In about ten minutes, I was able to stop shaking and crying. He told me that I knew that the most painful part of my heart was going to be touched and I was afraid. His calming voice helped me relax; I had nothing to be afraid of from this man. For the next two days, four hours each day, the horribly infected places that had been damaged in my heart as a child were opened up to Jesus. The counselor led me in prayer to take all the pain of abandonment and abuse to Jesus. Allowing Jesus to show me where He was and what He was doing in these moments. I cried through about eight hours.

The counselor talked and prayed with me through Dan repeating to me whatever the counselor would say. This process caused Dan and me to emotionally connect with each other because we were involved together in the painful healing process. My heart had emotionally locked before I had reached the age of one. Jesus showed me that if Dan would put one hand on my face, the other hand in the middle of my back, and hold me, this would comfort me and bring me peace and security. I hardly had been held when I was a baby. This action has been simple and yet powerfully therapeutic for me.

On the third day, the counselor took Dan in prayer to Jesus. For three hours, Dan cried out the pain of his heart. Dan saw a picture of Jesus holding my hand as a little girl in the back of a church sanctuary. He saw himself as a little boy standing in the front of the sanctuary looking at the two of us. Jesus and I began to walk towards Dan, and Jesus held out His hand towards Dan. Dan began to cry and said he did not know what to do. He was afraid. The counselor asked Dan, "What do you want to do?" Dan responded by saying that he wanted to take Jesus' hand. When Dan reached out his hand, Jesus embraced him in a hug. Dan cried and shook as I held him; during this moment, he was seeing this picture in his heart. Dan for the first time in his life was experiencing that God was real and that he, Dan, was seeing Him with the eyes of his heart. He knew that Jesus wanted a personal, one-on-one relationship with Dan. Dan saw Jesus walk with him to a running creek and sit down, asking Dan to sit with Him. He told Dan that He could come to the creek whenever he needed or wanted to and Jesus would sit with him and spend time talking with him. Whatever Dan wanted to talk about is what they would discuss. Dan's heart was healed from some incidents that happened to him as a young boy emotionally and spiritually. He realized he had been performing his whole life to prove that he was a man able to make his own decisions about his life.

God recognized him as the man He had created. God wanted to walk beside this man and be in relationship with him. God was not going to take over and run his life. He wanted to love Dan and have Dan love Him. It was the desire of my heart to see this breakthrough come in Dan's heart and life. I had known that there was something keeping Dan from feeling and seeing things with his heart. I had hoped with all my heart that this counselor could help him get free. I did not know that Jesus would be playing the major role in setting Dan free. After this week of counseling, Dan and I were emotionally connected in a way that we could not be pulled apart.

The connection has continued to this day. This connection has brought healing into my life and emotional well being. Dan cares for my heart because he understands how I need tenderness and reassurance of his commitment to me. As a child, I had gone through the traumas of abandonment, rejection, neglect, humiliation, betrayal, emotional detachment, insensitivity—along with ongoing physical, sexual, spiritual, and emotional abuse. I was under pressure from dominating control, performance-based acceptance, and withheld love. I was not talked to or communicated with about any situation that was happening in my childhood. I was traumatized by the many changes that came into my life. This environment locked my heart, and I could not relate to my family or others with my heart; instead I related only intellectually—with my head. God never intended us to use only our heads in making decisions. His biggest decision to give His Son, Jesus, to die for us was made with His heart of Love. "For God so loved the world, that He gave His only begotten Son, that whosoever believed on Him should not perish, but have everlasting life" (John 3:16). God acts out of His heart all of the time.

Out of the damaged emotions of my heart came spiritual issues into my life. These were fear, bitterness, legalism, defiance, pride, moral failure, hypocrisy, and temporal values. Once the emotional issues of my heart were healed and resolved, the spiritual issues were no longer a problem.

It was as if they disappeared. The spiritual issues had been there because I could not trust God with my heart. I am not saying I never sinned again, but I am saying I did not enjoy sin, and my heart would grieve when I did sin. I would run to my Father to find out why I had chosen to do wrong. He patiently and lovingly would show me why. Sin is always rooted in a wound in my heart or a false belief about God. In my heart I had believed many lies about God, and they continue to rise to the surface like dross rises from hot gold. When my life gets heated up by situations or pressures, sin sometimes comes to the surface, but along with it come the lies and wounds. When I take my sin to God, He reveals the lies and wounds, the dross is taken out, and what remains is pure gold.

I used to believe that God was sadistic. Sadistic means to derive pleasure or profit from someone else's pain. This was my conclusion as to why God allowed such abuse and trauma in my life as a little girl. I did not realize that Satan, the enemy both of God and my soul, was the sadistic one. He caused these traumas through the sin of other people's lives to come into mine in order to deceive me about God. He did not ever want me to know the Good News, which is that God is loving, good, and full of mercy and grace toward me. Therefore, I had to meet my own needs. My heart was in survival mode, and I was greedy in meeting my own needs. Survival means there is never enough beyond this moment, so you had better get extra when you can for the day is coming when there will not be any more to grab. I had been locked in bondage to survival, bound and determined to survive—no matter what it took.

Process of My Healing

The beginning of the process was a relationship with the living God. I had to believe that God existed, that He loved me, and that He meant me no harm, only goodness and mercy. God had His way of bringing healing into my life. It was not to be in the same exact way He would bring someone else healing. I am a unique human being, and unique situations had occurred in my life. God is the only one who totally understands my uniqueness. His goals are the same for others. To heal the wounds of their hearts, cause the sin to not be needed or desired, and bring them into a living relationship with Himself. But the way He heals them will be unique to them and their own life environment. "Slave Market Day" gives the understanding of why God redeems a person. It is purely because He wants to love them and be in a walking, talking, and understanding relationship with them. He desires to bless them by providing all they need to live here in this fallen world. He also wants others to be drawn to know Him through the life and love lived out through His children. This is why the *angel* people were so vital to my life. They gave me hope to carry on in the darkness. Hope that there was love somewhere in this world. Children of God become light for those who are still in darkness.

There are emotional ways I was damaged or wounded in my heart. Here is a list and the definition of each area of my emotional damage:

- Abandonment: Nine times I was left behind, disowned, withdrawn from, given up for adoption, and not chosen by "parents."

- Neglect: I was not cared for physically and emotionally; I was paid no attention, forgotten, and not talked to about life changes.

- Disregard: I was overlooked, passed over, excluded, ignored, and left to myself. I was a nobody.

- Insensitivity: I was treated apathetically, indifferent—never asked how I was feeling or doing. My grades in school should have spoken loudly to someone. No one in leadership ever sat down with me to talk about anything at the school.

- Humiliation: I was disgraced, shamed, degraded, embarrassed, and made fun of for wetting the bed.

- Betrayal: My trust was let down and broken in every parent I knew. I was turned in and threatened the few times I did try to speak out. I saw abuses go unheeded, unheard of, or not dealt with by those in authority.

- Despisement: I felt condemned, disliked, unwanted, discarded, detested, dirty, and rejected. I felt like my goal in life was to be good and perform well, but I never could make anyone satisfied with my behavior.

- Disrespect: Through emotional, physical, spiritual, and sexual abuse, I was ridiculed, put to shame, humiliated, and treated roughly. My body was abused physically and sexually. I was used for others' sexual pleasure and satisfaction against my will when I was too young to understand what was happening. I was controlled by dominance and punishment. My spirit was abused emotionally. Spiritually, I was force to live by biblical principles and rules without love, which caused rebellion in my heart.

- Emotional Detachment: I lived with people who were incapable of loving me; they couldn't give me love nor could they receive my love. I emotionally detached from feelings when it came to relationships with people.

- Replacement: I was replaced with new children or with a new job. I was replaced with someone more prettier or smarter than I.

Every person has a main emotional core issue, an issue of the heart that causes a person to react to situations and people in their life. If a person knows what their issue is, they can see how it has threaded itself throughout their whole life and controlled them. I have three sub-issues in my life. They are abandonment, replacement, and abuse. I believe my main emotional core issue is neglect: nobody taking action against abuse or the abuser. I can look back over my life and see how my emotional stability was damaged whenever someone abandoned or replaced me. But if I saw or knew that someone was being taken advantage of or abused, my heart was greatly damaged. This included no one taking action to help the person being abused. Also, no person stopped the abuser and took action against them. My relationship with God was affected because I was angry at Him for not taking action against the abusers and rescuing me.

As the counselor began to work with me, he had me face my husband, who became the closest care partner of my healing. Dan would hold my hands, and at any time I could lean my head on his shoulder. He would embrace me if I began to sob or needed his support emotionally.

The counselor spoke everything to Dan, and then my husband would repeat it to me. This enabled Dan and I to emotionally connect with each other. This enabled me to not emotionally connect with the counselor.

The next step was for me to connect with Jesus, share, and ask Him questions. I would take a painful memory and tell Jesus about what happened. I asked Jesus how this incident had damaged my heart. Jesus would in turn give me a picture of the damage. Once He showed me a vineyard full of grapes; the gate was left open. A huge crowd of people entered the vineyard and stomped all through the grapes and completely destroyed the entire place. Jesus reminded me that the vine was still intact because the root system was buried under the ground; it was possible for new branches and new grapes to grow if someone would clean up and care for the vineyard. He said that He would be that someone along with Dan, my husband. I saw Jesus very tenderly begin to pick up all the broken pieces. He asked me to forgive the abusers. As I took each abuser by name and each situation of abuse, I would ask Jesus to show me the damage done to my heart. I would then, by choice of my will, choose to forgive the abuser for the abuse. I would begin to feel the pain and cry.

As this was happening, I would ask Jesus to take the pain out of my heart and bring me peace. Immediately I felt the pain leave and peace come in. I felt bitterness and hate go out of my heart. I did not go through this process all in one day. The healing happened over a period of time because of the amount of abuse and trauma I had experienced. A memory would come to me during the day. I knew that Jesus wanted to talk with me about that abuse or traumatic event, so it was a cleansing process that has taken time.

My heart locked up emotionally at six months of age because of a spiritual and physically abusive traumatic happening in my life at the time. I remembered the incident in segments when I was forty-six years of age. A baby of six months cannot comprehend what is happening around or to them. Putting the pieces together when I was older helped me understand what had taken place. I cannot fully explain how this happens. I can only say that in a time frame of three months, parts of my blocked memory came back in bits and pieces like a puzzle. When I put all the pieces of the puzzle together, the memory returned. With my adult mind I could tell what had taken place at six months of age. This process involved the work of the Holy Spirit. He knew just when to give me a piece of the puzzle. It was given slowly and separately, so that I could handle the traumatic revelation. Some of the memory pieces were given during prayer or a counseling session, part in a dream of which I remember every detail, parts of my memory came as I was watching a movie or video clip, and some came during a conference. God used many ways to speak to me; I was willing to let Him out of my box of what He can and cannot do. He even arranged for the memory to be restored when many people around me could help me emotionally handle remembrance. I even have experienced post-traumatic stress with panic and anxiety attacks due to the memory. I have worked through these with praying, standing on the truths I have learned, and also with a small amount of medicine taken during the attacks.

Forgiveness of the abuser and those in authority over me was done for my own emotional healing. It was letting them off my hook for their actions. My soul was untied with theirs so that I could live free. I was accepting that what had happened to me was wrong and that it should not have happened. I understood how their sin had damaged me and how that damage affected me over the years. I was coming to accept the person that I am today because of the abuse and trauma I endured. I was accepting the consequences to my life due to their actions. I was turning their actions and fates over to a God who could deal justly with my abusers. I gave up my claim to make them pay for their debt against me. I was giving that responsibility to God to handle them in His way and timing. This allowed the damage of anger, judgment, and pain to leave my soul. This allowed hate to leave my heart, which was replaced by peace and grace. I began to act out of a peaceful, loving, and grace-filled heart. I had a heart of mercy and understanding; I had compassion in situations with people I dealt with on a daily basis.

I still struggle whenever I see abuse that is being neglected.

I feel like I have to take action in some way to prevent any more abuse. I still struggle with not retaliating against abuse in wrong ways. I am continuing to allow God to show me when I am *reacting* instead of *responding* to a situation of abuse. This is why I know this is the emotional core issue of my heart. It still remains my greatest weakness. I am still working through post-traumatic stress, anxiety, and panic attacks. I have to continue to stand on the truth of God, that He has given me a sound mind and not a spirit of fear.

I also had to face and deal in my heart with my own wrong actions. I believe those wrong actions were done out of a childish heart trying to survive in a world gone wrong. I look closely at my actions and attitudes these days to see what my motivation is behind them. Motivation of the heart is the standard with which I believe God looks at the heart of a person. God knew that a lot of my wrong actions and attitudes were due to the damage that had been done to me. He sees and knows all about me. As my husband and I have met with people and helped them get their hearts healed of damage, the wrong attitudes and actions in their lives disappear. We do take them through a process of acknowledging, renouncing, and repenting of those wrong actions and attitudes. This is called taking responsibility for your own life. Whenever I see Dan or myself reacting to a situation, instead of responding, we search to find out what is behind the reaction. We ask questions of each other to see what feelings we were having and why. We emotionally care for each other by sitting and searching out the issue.

Recently, Dan and I were at our daughter's basketball game and the play was getting rough. The girls were hitting and bumping each other, and girls were getting knocked to the ground. I was getting upset because of my abuse issue. All of a sudden I realized that Dan was shrinking back against the wall and getting very quiet. I turned to him to ask if he was okay, but I could tell he was not. I suggested that we go and get a drink in the lobby. Later, we realized that his emotional core issue was getting touched also. Conflict in any way is his emotional core issue.

Where Dan attended high school, there were racial riots; when these happened, all the students and teachers had to literally run for their lives. Dan was a small-framed kid, unable to defend himself against the bigger, meaner students. His personality has always been gentle and kind. He has a memory block of most of his junior and senior high school years. These school riots traumatized Dan severely. Whenever Dan gets into a conflict, he tends to run for his life or try to get out of it somehow. It scares him. The basketball game was getting to be too much for him; it was creating conflict between the players and the parents on the sidelines. Also, I was making it worse, because I wanted to stop the abuse that was going on—my reaction was adding more conflict to the situation. We sat down that evening and talked to each other gently and quietly. We prayed and asked Jesus to bring healing to Dan's heart concerning the riots and the damage that had happened to his heart. As a result, Dan and I understand the emotional core issue of each other's heart. We can more easily love and give attention to areas of the heart that have been damaged.

Belief & Theology of God

The foundation for what I now believe about God comes from my journey of searching for the truth about who God is really. I had to begin the search for myself. If I had just believed what had been taught me, He would not be my God. He would be my parents' God, or the preachers' God, or the Bible college's God. I had to reach out myself to really come to know the truth about God. I had to ask, "Will the real God please stand up for me?" Now that I have come into contact with the living God, a relationship with God is what keeps me growing in Him more. I read the Bible a lot as a young person and had a basic understanding of it by the time I was out of college. But my reading of the Bible was misconstrued because of the glasses of my childhood. When I read the Bible, I read judgment and condemnation. Now as I read the Bible, verses jump out at me that I never saw before; they tell me that God is for me and is full of mercy and grace. The Scriptures come alive and I hear God speaking to me in my heart as I read.

One day, in the middle of a crisis in my life, I decided to try God out. I started talking to Him to see if He really existed or if those people in my life had just made Him up. I thought, *This Bible tells of a pretty awesome God, and if He is real, I want to know Him.* Something started happening—God started talking back to me. He answered me by giving me understanding and awareness of things I never had wisdom about before. He answered by coincidences suddenly happening. I would say in my mind to Him what I needed, and the next day it would be provided for out of the blue. I had not told anyone else what I was thinking. Now this could have been coincidence, except that it happened too often. I would ask Him a question, and a book would "appear" that would explain the answer to my question. He never came at me in an angry or impatient way. He never made me feel like I was stupid. He knew I was a child and needed to be trained. I listened and began to ask Him questions about what I wanted to understand about Him. He answered me through directing me to the Bible, other Christians, messages from speakers, retreats, and even through the books I was using to teach the girls their schooling. The answers came the same day, the next week or month, maybe in a year, but there has not been one that has gone unanswered.

I once asked Him to explain the Trinity to me. By the Trinity, I mean that God the Father, God the Son, and God the Holy Spirit are all one (I John 5:7). I asked Him, "How can you be three persons and yet still be one God?" He showed me a picture of the physical heart and how it has four valves. Each valve has a different purpose, but it takes all the valves to complete the heart and cause it to function. There are three persons in the Godhead and each has a different function or purpose. But the three complete Him whom we call God. No one else knew I was asking God these questions, so I knew that only God could bring me an answer.

I had heard statements my whole life, for instance, the plan of salvation. So one day I got out a tract that explained the plan of salvation for people to read. I took the tract to God one afternoon, and asked Him to explain this tract to me. God helped me to understand things so that I could understand them as a child. Jesus said that we need to become as a child to receive the kingdom of God. Here is the explanation God gave to bring me understanding about the plan of salvation.

God totally and completely embodies love. He is love (I Corinthians 13) and light (I John 1:5). He cannot sin or in a wrongful way get His needs met. He always acts out love for the benefit of others. He created people to give them His love, but He does not force upon them His love. They must make a choice to receive His love. Love is only true love when a person makes the choice to give or receive love. God gave Adam and Eve this choice through the tree of the Knowledge of Good and Evil. He put the tree in the garden and then told them not to eat of the fruit of this tree. God loved them, and He wanted Adam and Eve to love Him by trusting in Him and believing what He said about the fruit on the tree. He told them that the fruit would cause them to die. This tree would bring them knowledge that would kill them. An enemy of God through a serpent in the garden deceived Eve into eating from the tree that God had warned them not to eat. He caused her to believe that God was withholding wisdom from her that would allow her to become like God. Well, who wouldn't want to be God? He was a pretty awesome being. Adam did not stop Eve from eating the fruit, even though he was right there at the time (Genesis 3:6). Adam chose to also eat the fruit when Eve turned and offered it to him. This tree gave them the knowledge of the difference between good and evil. It was a knowledge that they could not handle because they were not God. Adam and Eve chose to distrust what God had said; they ate fruit from the tree. The fruit did cause them to die, both spiritually and physically. God quickly removed them from the garden so that they would not eat from the tree of Eternal Life and live forever in this condition of death and darkness. They were in darkness because they were removed from the presence of God whose life was the light of men (John 1:4). God loved Adam and Eve who are the representatives of the human race or the World. Out of his heart of love, God provided a way for the human race to come back into an eternal relationship with Him (Colossians 1:13).

When we do evil in order to get our needs met, we are sinning against God's law of love. Our selfish wrongdoing puts a wall of darkness between God and us. God's life and light cannot reach our existence. This darkness prevents us from being in relationship with God. "For in God there is no darkness" (I John 1:5). Selfishness or wrongdoing cannot go unpunished, or it would mean that it is okay for us to get our needs met in a wrong way. Our selfishness ends in death; it is a disease that keeps growing and spreading. Our sin hurts others, who then turn to hurt us back or hurt someone else by their selfishness or wrongdoing. This all ends in death, darkness, and destruction in our lives. God wanted to remove the death, darkness, and destruction for us. He gave His own Son, Jesus, that the world would not perish, but would be able to come back into relationship with Him and receive life and light into their existence.

Jesus came to earth through the conception of the Holy Spirit, who is God, and a woman named Mary. Jesus was God and He was human. Because He was God, He was love. He came to earth and lived thirty-three years without choosing to do something selfish or wrong even one time. He chose to walk in relationship with His Father God and fulfill the will of God for His life's purpose here on this earth. God's will for His Son was to fulfill the whole Law that had been set forth by God and to also take our punishment of death for our sins and selfishness. He paid the price for the sins of all humankind. This payment took away the punishment of death, the wall of darkness, and opened a way for humankind to come back into the relationship of light and eternal life of God. Jesus was able to pay our sin debt because He never entered that darkness by sinning Himself.

Every human has chosen to act selfishly by meeting their own needs in a wrong way. None of us have been able to keep the whole law. This is what God knew about us whenever He told Adam and Eve not to eat of the Tree of Knowledge of Good and Evil. Some of these wrong ways are killing, stealing, adultery, telling lies, coveting, jealousy, disrespect for parents, etc. Every human needs Jesus to pay their punishment of death for them in order that they may be saved from perishing in their darkness. Jesus' sacrifice of His own life allows every human to be able to come back into relationship with God the Father. This brings them back into the life, light, and love of God. Every human is given the choice to choose Jesus as their Savior and believe that God wants to walk in relationship with them. Choice is the key to love becoming true love. God does not force us out of our darkness. He does pursue and woo us through many different ways to come to Him. Through the telling of this *good news,* so that people can know of His love for them. Through people who have already come into the light and love of God, such as the *angels* in my life. When the angels came to the shepherds on the night Jesus was born to Mary, they came sharing *good news* and bringing peace on earth from God's good will toward us. Jesus was God's free gift of love to humankind that they may once again receive His light, love, and life. He does not just want to be our Creator. He wants to be our Father and cause us to become His children. Children inherit the Father's estate. For God, that estate is love. So just as Adam and Eve were given a choice in the garden to believe God, we are now each of us given a choice to believe and receive God's way back into light and eternal life.

There is another part of this story, though. God has an enemy. The enemy of God is an angel who also was created by God. This angel decided one day that he wanted to be God himself. He was jealous and coveted God's throne of authority and power. He wanted to be worshiped as God was worshiped. He rebelled against God's authority, like a toy with the ability to talk and walk that decides it wants to be the designer, inventor, and machine that made the toy in the first place. This enemy's name was Satan. He stirred up the other angels to help him go up against God in order to take over heaven and rule. God in His wisdom and love knew that the angel did not have what it took to rule in His place and said, "No." This enemy decided to go to war with God. God won the battle and proceeded to throw this angel of selfishness and rebellion out of His own presence of love. God allowed this angel to continue to exist, only because He wanted to come into a real relationship of love with humankind. The enemy knows that God gives us a choice.

In order for humans to make a choice they had to be given two choices. The enemy's choice is to be a god yourself, make your own decisions, and act independent of God and His love. So, Satan continues to deceive humans into believing they do not need God or, as in my case and Eve's, He deceives people into believing that God is withholding from them and causing all their darkness. He deceives us subtly. He does not want humans to come to know who God really is and that God loves them. Satan is continuing the battle for God's throne here on the earth among humans. He rules out of a kingdom of darkness and deception. He wants to kill, steal, and destroy everyone so that God's kingdom of love will be destroyed. He does not want any human to know the good news. We cannot be forced to love or it is no longer love. God is love. Love is walking in a relationship of trust, faithfulness, patience, kindness, joy, peace, goodness, gentleness, and self-control. We each have to make this choice. No one can make it for us. We must each hear the good news, believe it, and choose to receive the free gift of God's Son. Receiving the free gift brings us into a relationship as sons and daughters of God. Thus, we inherit our Father's kingdom of love and all that goes with that inheritance. The reason we share the Gospel, is to share the good news that there is a true living God who loves us and cares about each of us personally. He has provided a way for all people through Jesus. A way for them to survive, to be saved, and to live an abundant life as children of God. God does not want to be just our Creator, He wants us to belong to Him in a way that can never be severed or changed. God not only saves us for heaven someday, but He also saves us for the present, to walk with us in relationship here in the fallen world where we are living. Satan knows of our worth to God. The price God had to pay to get us out of Satan's kingdom of darkness was the death of His only Begotten Son. Begotten means to bring forth and, in this case, to bring forth a son child. It means to obtain by effort. God gave up the life of His dearly beloved Son to pay the price of death for us to be able to become His sons and daughters also. He had to watch as His own Son died a cruel death by the very people He wanted to save.

I had been parenting my daughters under the very law that caused Adam and Eve to die. It was as though I was feeding them the fruit of the Tree of Knowledge of Good and Evil. It was killing them and my relationship with their hearts. In my relationship with my daughters, I did not just want to be the woman who conceived and gave birth to them. I also wanted a much deeper relationship with them as mother and daughter. I wanted to pour my love into their lives, and I desired that they choose to love me in return. To force my girls to obey, respect, and choose to love me just because I had given birth to them was impossible. Using the basis of who we are or our authority over someone to get them to obey, respect, or love us are the root causes of rebellion in the heart. My daughters needed love through relating to the girls in their hearts by fellowship and understanding. Working through life's situations with them side-by-side. Because this never occurred in my life through a parental relationship, I did not know to do this with my children.

With my birth mother, upon meeting her for the first time, I had no emotional heart connection. Therefore, I felt no emotion because there was no relationship between us. She could not reach out to me and hug me; because in order not to hurt during all those years of separation, she had shut down her heart towards me. After I hugged her, she cried. My hug was a sign of my forgiveness towards her abandonment of me. Forgiveness was the love and light of God penetrating her heart so that she could let her heart feel love toward me again. The desire of her heart when she gave me up was that one day we would be reunited. But without relationship all those years, I did not feel anything towards this woman, even though she had conceived and given me birth.

It is the same way with God. He is our creator, but without knowing Him through relationship, our hearts do not intertwine with His and we cannot respect, obey, or choose to love Him. Compounded upon that is the way the enemy deceives us into believing lies about God. We believe in our hearts that God is against us, not for us. I could not trust God with everyday life situations because of the damage I believed He had allowed others to do to me. I could not give Him my respect or obedience, let alone my heart. But there came a point that I knew I could do nothing with the shattered pieces of my heart; I decided to let Jesus have my heart because I had no use for it anymore.

Like the items I would put in a garage sale. The items to

me are not worth keeping any longer, so I sell them to whoever comes along and does see some worth in them. So much worth that they would pay the price for the item that I am asking. God came along and paid the price because He saw worth in my heart. God then moved into my heart. He made my heart His home. Jesus' death made this possible because He became my righteousness. God took each shattered piece and began to wash and clean them. It was a painful but gentle process. The pieces were as hard as stone. No truth can penetrate a heart of stone. In a real heart, when a person dies, blood no longer can flow through the heart because there is no life. It eventually hardens as a rock from the lack of the life's blood flowing through. Jesus poured His antibiotic of unconditional love onto the pieces of my heart. He cleaned the infection out with His grace, and the pieces became soft and tender. He began to put the pieces together with the special bonding glue of loving heart relationship and training.

Damaged Heart

Jesus brought the healed heart to me and asked me to begin to live out of this new heart. As I began to live out of my heart in relationship to the Father, I found that when fear came, the presence of God and truth would also come and cause the fear to go away. This truth was the light of God's reality. God's answers to all my questions, my identity of being His daughter, verses from the Bible, songs, pictures, and also *angel* memories. This truth could penetrate into my new heart that was soft and alive. The scars remained in my heart. The scars represent all that God has healed my heart from. They testify to what God has done.

Healed Heart

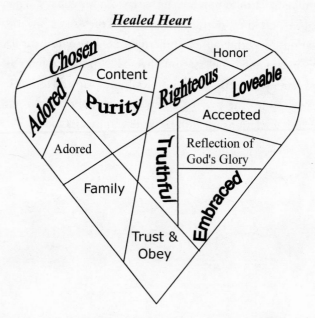

As I began to walk in this relationship with God as His daughter, I grew to trust Him more and more with the details of my life. I soon became aware of the survival mode and greediness of my heart. It was causing me to do wrong things to myself and others in order to get my needs met. I no longer had the desire to do wrong. I wanted to find out what was causing me to do wrong. This is when God began to show me how the enemy, through other people's lives, had tried to destroy my heart and my understanding of who He was as God.

In summary, God's plan is to save us from the enemy's kingdom of darkness and bring us back into a family relationship with Himself that is an indwelling and eternal one (Colossians 1:13). He enabled this plan through His Son coming to earth to purchase us back from the enemy. When we hear and know of this *good news*, and turn and come into relationship with God, His inheritance of love automatically becomes ours and blesses our lives. His presence indwells and parents us. This love and blessing in turn flows out of our lives into the lives of others, pursues, and woos them towards a relationship with the true and living God.

Damaged Closed Heart

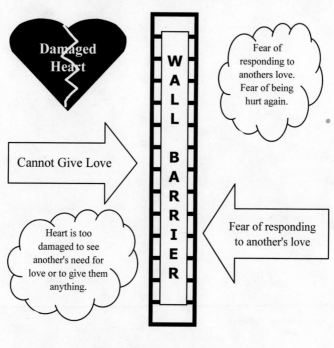

Damaged Heart

W A L L   B A R R I E R

Fear of responding to anothers love. Fear of being hurt again.

Cannot Give Love

Heart is too damaged to see another's need for love or to give them anything.

Fear of responding to another's love

Open Responsive Heart

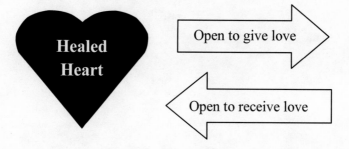

Healed Heart

Open to give love

Open to receive love

FROM THE HEART OF MY HUSBAND

As I neared the finish of this book, it was suggested that I include a chapter in telling Dan's perspective of his own heart's journey. We both readily agreed that this was not only a great suggestion, but also a vital part to the whole story. Dan grew up with very loving and responsible parents. His dad worked and provided a good living for his wife and five children. He spent time teaching his children in many areas of life, such as taking care of their vehicles, financial accountability, etc. He took the family on many fun trips and taught his sons to hunt and fish. His mother stayed at home, caring for the children and their home. Dan never had a day where he went hungry or was abused in his home. His home was a place of safety and security. Dan was the youngest of five children in their home. His parents took him to church his whole life and through this involvement encouraged Dan's spiritual growth in knowledge of God and the Bible. Dan lived with the same family, in the same house, and community his whole childhood. His family traveled to visit their grandparents at least two weekends a month a few hours away. His uncle had a farm on which Dan loved to hunt for many an hour for rabbits, squirrel, and quail.

Dan on the outside was happy, healthy, and content in

life. Contributing life factors, though, caused him to shut down his heart emotionally. In his heart, he was not sure what his identity was. As the baby of the family, he grew up with decisions made for him—the natural process of being the youngest in the family. He grew up following where everyone else was going or what they wanted to do. He was the youngest, so he was not asked for his opinion or choice in matters of decision. Whenever he hunted with his dad and brother, he was expected to follow their lead. Dan's personality and gifting in making decisions and expressing himself is done slowly, with planning and thought. People around him sometimes would take this as mental slowness and therefore did not wait around to see what he was thinking or processing into a plan or decision. Bitterness began to grow in his heart because he wanted to be valued for his thoughts and ideas.

Dan loved hunting. His favorite show was *Daniel Boone*. One day while hunting, when he was between eight and nine years old, a large covey of quail got up right in front of him. When a covey of quail gets up, they make a loud fluttering noise with all their wings going off at the same time; the movement of the birds can be quite startling. As a small kid, this sudden movement and noise startled and scared Dan to the point that he began to cry. His father turned to him and said, "Danny, if you are going to cry you need to go on back to the car, or you can quit crying and come hunting with us men." Dan was really scared and emotionally could not quit crying, so he turned around very upset and walked all the way back to the car. Unknown to his father, Dan's heart had been crushed. Emotionally, Dan believed two lies in his heart that day. One, that he didn't have what it took to be a man, and two, that real men do not get scared or cry. His dad nor Dan had any idea how Dan's heart had been affected that day.

A second contribution to the damage in Dan's heart was what happened in several of America's high schools in the seventies. Dan has a memory block of most of his junior and senior high school years. During these years violent racial riots took place in his school. Dan was small framed for his age and weighed a lot less than most of the guys in his school. Many times, gunshots would suddenly ring out, knives were thrown, and there was loud yelling and fighting. The school bell would ring, and this would mean only one thing to Dan: Run for your life! Get somewhere safe quick! Dan would dart out of the classroom and run as quickly as he could to get out of the building and out of harm's way. Dan went into survival mode mentally and emotionally disassociated, from the fear and trauma of the violence. No one knew how this was affecting Dan by causing him to shut down emotionally. This experience wrongly confirmed to Dan's heart once again that he was not a man because he would be scared and have to run. He did not see himself capable of defending himself or anyone else physically and emotionally. He felt threatened and would freeze up when he encountered conflict in any form.

The third contributing factor to Dan's heart issues is that he knew about God, but he did not understand the reality of knowing and walking in relationship with God. Dan grew up knowing that God and the Bible were right and true, and he believed intellectually and accepted Jesus as his Savior.

He attended a youth group at church and went to college at a Bible college. He went on mission trips and did a summer internship in Alaska working with the youth of a church. He did all of this with an intellectual, locked heart. By this I mean that Dan never in his heart emotionally connected with God by knowing him personally. He believed in God with his head but did not know Him in his heart. He literally did not have a genuine need for God. Dan's personality was gentle, kind, and serving. His outward actions caused people to believe he was living life out of a relationship with God. A person can look, act, sing, pray, and dress like a spirit-controlled Christian and actually be living out of their natural personality. Living out of this nature is living out of your own goodness and strengths, not by the leading of a relationship with God.

In the weeks that we spent with the counselor, Dan came to understand that he had never related to Jesus in his heart. Jesus came and showed Dan the three above issues that had locked him into an intellectual heart. Jesus revealed that Dan didn't know what his identity or value was as a person. He also showed Dan that domination by fear or force, slowness in expressing himself and making decisions, and being physically small all attributed to the damage in Dan's heart. Buried deep in his heart were these lies that he believed about himself that he did not want to ever be confirmed. This is why Dan took off to Alaska to prove, first of all, that he did have what it took to be a man; second, that he would never allow himself to be scared, but would conquer his fears; third, that he was a real man because he never cried. Dan disassociated emotionally into an intellectual mind-set.

He then would never feel the pain associated with his childhood. After Jesus came and embraced Dan, He replaced the lies with the truths about Dan. The truth is that God created Dan for a specific purpose. He created Dan with just the right physical frame, mental capabilities, and emotional heart of a man that could cry or be scared. God wanted to come into relationship with Dan and fulfill the purpose in and through Dan for which he was created. God alone knows what those purposes are, and only through coming into a heart relationship with God can Dan know and fulfill those purposes.

Dan could not care for me, his young bride, emotionally, only intellectually with his head. He did not know how to respond to my emotions of excitement, joy, tears, sadness, anger, disappointment, and fear. He had shut all of these emotions out of his life so that he could prove that he was a man. The only times he allowed himself to show emotion was when he had accomplished a manly accomplishment. Such as bear hunting, catching huge fish, and grand projects, at which he was very capable. These showed his value and manhood. Yet, none of these accomplishments were helping Dan to connect with God, his wife, and daughters in relationship.

Jesus came and unlocked the door to Dan's heart because Dan had come to the end of his own strength. He had told God, "Here I am with my arms outstretched, ready to do whatever it takes to really come into relationship with You, Birdie, and my daughters." Jesus removed the pain and lies from Dan's heart and restored it with love and truth. Dan came to realize his identity as a son of God, and that God created him with a specific purpose in mind. It is in the heart of Dan—the very center of a person—where God desires to make His dwelling place. In the Old Covenant, the Holy of Holies, was the inmost room of the temple and where the presence of God dwelt among His people. It was a picture of where God would dwell within men and women in the New Covenant through Jesus Christ. That dwelling place is in our hearts. It is when we allow the life of Jesus Christ to be lived out through our hearts that others, touched by God, are made able to see and believe in the living God.

Dan's core care statement is how I choose to care for his heart. "What if I, Birdie, choose to value you as a man and your decisions? What if I were to patiently wait for you to communicate your thoughts and ideas and not dominate or laugh at you? What if I choose to not put you in situations of conflict through pressure, but to communicate with you when you are not under pressure to perform and allow God to work through you to resolve issues of conflict? I will value you as the man God uses to lead our home and look to you for direction and leadership." As I choose to care for Dan, I see him walking as the man God made him to be. I hear wisdom and see leadership skills being developed. I see how God, through the Holy Spirit, directs our home through my husband, our leader. He responds to me emotionally with excitement, tears, peace, faithfulness, and expressions of his love. He cares about my heart's desires.

MINISTERING TO OTHERS
IN GOD'S PRESENCE

Caring for one another has enabled and given us the desire to reach out and help others find healing for their damaged hearts. Humility and unconditional love are the keys needed to reach out and help someone. God is the giver of these two keys. God knows each person individually. We ask Him to take over and guide us—to show us how we may join Him in helping that person each time we meet with someone. The emotional core issue of the person's heart is what we search for; it is at the center of all the damage in their hearts. Everything else flows from this core issue.

People come for counsel when they have found themselves unable to handle or control their lives. Asking them to describe what they find themselves reacting to in life's situations is where we begin. Their answers reveal clues as to the issue that is bothering them deeper in their hearts. Life happenings that are causing them to react in anger, bitterness, depression, or retaliation is a signal flag that the heart has been damaged. If the heart is well, the person can respond with reason, stability, and the giving and receiving of love. Severe reaction shows that there is severe wounding in the heart of a person. The heart must be opened up and the infected wound must be cleaned out in order for the heart to function properly. Jesus has the love and power that can cleanse and heal the wounds of the heart. He knows and understands every person's heart (Psalm 139). As we pray with and listen to the person share what is troubling them, the Holy Spirit guides us to ask the right questions and probe in the right places of the heart. We could not do this by ourselves—we do not have the complete knowledge about the person that God does.

We begin by caring for the person, regardless of the sin in their life. We have discovered that the sinful behavior is resolved whenever the heart becomes healed; the desire to sin is no longer there. We also help people resolve sin issues where they do struggle. We do not try to resolve the sin issues in the beginning of the process. Sin is an action usually taken by a person trying to get the wounds of their heart healed without the help of God. Sin is always related to a wound in the heart. Eve was wounded in her heart whenever she believed the lie that God was betraying her by withholding from her the ability to become like Him. The Bible says that Eve was the one in the transgression (I Timothy 2:14).

Here is an example out of my life. I stole food because as a child, my stomach was hungry and my hunger overruled any sense of right and wrong. I did know that I was taking what belonged to someone else, because I hid whenever I did the stealing. The adults in my life were committing evil against me by not feeding me correctly. Provide for me food, and I have no need or desire to take another's food. As a child I could maintain my innocence because I had no other means and did not have the knowledge to provide for my hunger other than stealing. But under the law, it was still hurting someone else, and therefore it was wrong—a sin. This hunger also created a wound in my soul, which caused survival to become an issue in my heart. I became a hoarder, a greedy soul. As an adult, I always had to maintain my food cupboard at full capacity. If we were out of money, I would begin to get stressed and angry and would hoard the groceries we did have. I would get upset if one of the girls would open a new bag of food without asking me first. I always shopped in large quantity. Food sometimes would spoil because we did not have time to eat all that I would buy.

When I recognized my wrong reactions to my girls, then I took the healing steps that Dan and I take with the people who come to us for counsel. First, I asked Jesus to show me the reason I was so upset that the bag of food was opened. He revealed to me my hunger issue as a child. I deserved to be fed as a child. My heart was wounded with the lie that I would have to take care of and provide for myself in this area of need. Second, I accepted that these people did wrong in withholding provision for me. Third, I asked Jesus to take this lie and pain out of my heart and replace it with His truth and peace. Fourth, Jesus asked me to forgive those people and allow Him to pay for their sin against me. I needed only to forgive them with my will. I did not have to *feel* like forgiving them. I chose to forgive them by name for not feeding me as a child. The pain of hunger left my heart. The infection was cleansed and my heart was healed. Peace came, and I no longer had the desire to hoard food and be greedy. The reality was that God my Father would make provision for me. He is Jehovah-Jireh, my provider. Now

I enjoy seeing my daughters open new bags of groceries. I actually find myself laughing and rejoicing. Especially if it is the last bag, because I know in my heart that God owns all the groceries in the world. I can stand on this truth because my heart knows it to be true.

Previously, the truth would not work in my life because it could not penetrate my heart because of all the infection and wounds. Part of the infection was the false ideas I had of God. My heart could not trust the truths or reality of God because down deep in my heart, I believed that God had caused all the trauma and abuse in my life. I could not trust God with my heart; to believe in what someone says, you have to be able to trust that person. To stand on truth when you have no proof is foolishness. Even when a person sits in a chair, he does so because he has seen others sit in a chair before—it held them up, so he believes it will hold him up. The only person who had faith in sitting in a chair was the inventor of the chair, and he probably knew the science of the chair and that it could hold up under the pressure of his body's weight. God is a God who makes Himself known to us before He asks us to believe in Him. He comes in a way to prove that He is who He says He is. To Moses, it was the burning bush that gave credence to his heart that God really was the I AM. He does not ask us to believe blindly that He is the Almighty God. False, dead gods demand this because they cannot prove they exist. If a person worships or believes in a god that does not make contact with them, then they are adoring a false, dead god.

God does ask us to trust Him and step out in faith after He has established relationship with us. Belief in God comes through a relationship that has already been established through hearing the *gospel* message. In sending Jesus down to earth to become man, God established contact with us. Jesus came to bring us into relationship with His Father God. As God's children, we are also here on earth to draw people who are still living in darkness to our Father God. If we draw people to ourselves, then we eventually disappoint them because we are not God. So we take people to Jesus and let Him lead them into relationship with their Father God. Jesus takes over the healing process.

I always thought prayer was getting alone somewhere, kneeling, and saying speeches to God. After reading the book of Psalms in the Bible, God revealed that David was shepherding his sheep out in a huge pasture, running from his enemies, face down in caves, and hungry as he yelled or cried out to God in prayer. God showed me that I too could talk to Him anytime and anywhere. I began to act as though God was with me wherever I went. I have this ongoing conversation with Him. I bring Him into every area of my life and treat Him like He is my best friend.

Remember my best girlfriend that I had such good times with earlier in my childhood? This is how she and I developed a relationship. Talking, spending time together, and doing activities together. Looking at clouds or sunsets, rainbows, and even playing in the rain together. We got to know and love each other's hearts. I would have told her any secret in my heart. I would have given my life for her. She was my friend and I was her friend. My heart intertwined with hers and hers with mine. But in order for that process to begin, I had to walk over to her door, knock, and wait for an answer. The door may not have ever opened, but it did. I told her that I had a purple bicycle like hers. That I wanted her to ride to school with me that day. I was offering her my friendship. She accepted my offer with a glad heart.

God knocked on the door first through the sending of His son, Jesus. Because of my childhood readings about God, and the *angels* in my life that had shown me God's love, a tiny mustard seed of faith had been planted in my lonely heart. I was compelled to go open the door to see if He was really there and really the God I had read about. He was there when I got to the door, and He was beside Himself with excitement that I responded to His knock. I found out that He was more than I had ever thought or imagined Him to be. We began to spend time together, and He let me set the schedule. Sometimes He would knock, but if I was too busy, He didn't get impatient or upset. He would patiently come back again another time. I miss Him when I don't spend time with Him. He is just like my best girlfriend. When she moved away, I thought I was going to die, because my heart grieved over the loss of her friendship. Once a heart experiences relationship with God, it keeps coming back because of His faithfulness. Talking to God and Jesus is easy. It is expressing myself to Him in just the same way I would express myself to a good friend. I just get real and talk normal. I do not get all dressed up and look perfect before I talk to Him.

Dan and I lead people to talk to Jesus, and He often responds to them with a word picture, song, memory, verse, or an analogy that He knows they understand. Something like the vineyard picture I described earlier. One day we were praying with an auto mechanic who washed his old, red truck every other day. He asked God if He was clean in God's sight after resolving the sin of moral failure in his life. All of a sudden this big guy grins and relays the picture that God was giving to his heart. He sees a picture of his old, red truck going into the power carwash; when it came out on the other side, it was a shiny, brand new red truck. He had always dreamed in his heart of owning a brand new red truck. He understood clearly in his heart what God was saying to Him. He was as clean, new, and perfect as the new truck that had just come through the power wash. God always finds a way to communicate with us uniquely.

The Holy Spirit is the leader in the counseling times. When people share with us what has damaged their hearts, we ask for and listen to see if God is showing us something in particular. We put ourselves in their shoes and try to understand how they felt when the damage was happening to them. This is what Jesus did by living here and then going to the cross. This is why He can be our intercessor and priest before our Father in Heaven. The abuse I went through enables me to more easily understand people's pain. We simply take them through the same steps we have gone through ourselves. We ask them questions, and when the timing seems right we begin to lead them to Jesus by talking to Him and asking Him questions. We have listed here some of the prayers we use. They repeat after us the prayers.

Jesus,

This is (the person's name). Do You have time for me?

Do You care about me? Do You love me? Can You help me?

How are You different than (the person who damaged my heart)?

Could You show me what my heart looks like from the damage that has been done?

Could You show me the walls that I have built to protect my heart?

Where is my heart? Will You heal my heart?

What do You like about me?

Where were You when this happened to me?

How did this abuse damage my heart?

As we ask Jesus these questions, there is usually an answer in the form of a picture that comes into their mind. This picture is something that speaks directly to the person's heart uniquely. If the person is locked in their heart towards God spiritually, they usually feel safe to pray to Jesus. God will speak through bringing memories or songs the person remembers. After each question, we pause and allow the person to share what God has shown them. Whenever the person begins to cry, we know that God has touched their heart and the pain inside. We ask Jesus to bring peace and remove the pain from their heart. When the pain is gone, then the crying stops—this is evidence that healing occurred. We teach them how to take each point of damage to Jesus, allowing Him to heal the damage, take the pain and equip the individual to forgive the offender. Then their heart is healed and they begin to smile. They are able to give and receive love. Their heart has come to new life and freedom.

PRAYERS FOR RESOLVING EMOTIONAL ISSUES

Resolving Abandonment Pain

Jesus, I felt so hurt when my mother abandoned the family when I was four years of age. I really needed a mother. Jesus, can you draw me a picture of how my heart was damaged by my mothers absence? Jesus, do you want me to open my heart to trust my husband? Is his heart open to love and accept me? Jesus, how would I open my heart to him? How would I begin to respond to allowing him to love me? Jesus, what would our marriage be like if I was able to respond to love and give love?

Resolving Neglect

Jesus, my parents never focused on me or paid attention to me. I played by myself alone and no one seemed to care about me. I felt alone, uncared for and neglected. Jesus, do you care about little boys who never get love? Jesus, do you love me? Jesus, could you draw me a picture of what my heart looked like neglected by each of my family members? Jesus could you bring peace to my heart? Jesus, do you want me to open my heart to trust relationship with my wife? How would I open my heart to her? Jesus, how would I feel love for the first time? Do you want me to enjoy it?

Resolving Being Ignored

Jesus, my father emotionally ignored me when I was growing up. He never responded when I wanted to talk. He always seemed to be reading or busy and never had any time for me. Jesus, are you like my father to not have time for me or are you different? How are you different? Jesus, how was I damaged emotionally by his ignoring me? Jesus, can you heal my heart and bring peace there? Jesus, what do you want me to do if I am ignored again?

Resolving Being Disowned

Jesus, I was conceived before my parents were married causing my parents to feel that they had to get married. They always blamed me and never connected to care for me. Jesus, how did that damage my heart? Jesus, do you discard a child you created? Jesus, did you want me and that's why you didn't allow me to be aborted? Jesus, can you heal the pain I feel inside because I was disowned?

Resolving Emotional Detachment

Jesus, my parents didn't know how to meet my emotional needs for love. I never felt love from them. Jesus, do you care? Jesus, can you draw me a word picture of how my heart looks like damaged? Jesus, how can you heal my heart? Jesus do you want me to respond to feeling loved by my husband? Jesus, do you love me?

When I opened up to Jesus about the traumatic beating I took one night, followed by sitting and listening to the Bible being read by the same man who had beaten me, Jesus spoke healing words into my heart. I asked Him where He was that night. He showed me the other children's faces as they watched me being beaten and they cried in their hearts for me. He heard their cries just as He had heard Abel's blood cry out and the children of Israel cry out when they were in bondage. He told me that He was in those children's hearts, and He was crying out to the Father in intercession for me. He then told me that He was inside of me; He felt and experienced with me all that I had gone through that night. He felt the beating, the humiliation, the broken heart, the spiritual abuse, and the rejection. He knew exactly what I had gone through. I knew then that Jesus did live inside of me; He described all that took place that night. I asked Him why He allowed me to suffer. He said it had to be so because of the free will of man to choose to love and trust God or to rebel and sin and disobey God through damaging a little girl's body and soul. He also told me that God never wastes pain and suffering. He said that His life in me was a reflection of the glory of God's love.

A rainbow surrounds the throne of God (Revelation 4:3). That rainbow is a reflection of His glory (Ezekiel 1:26-28). He said that a rainbow of color would reflect through what has happened and a pot of gold would be at the end of the rainbow. God's Word was confirmed to me when I found out several weeks later that in a gold-mining operation, whenever they are drilling and hit gold, a rainbow of color sparks out of the rock. Thus the saying, there is a pot of gold at the end of a rainbow. My heart received healing through His words. I always loved rainbows, and God continues to talk with me through them. The rebellion against God left my heart, as I began to understand that God has a purpose and plan that stands above anything that happens to me here on this earth.

Tell it to Jesus	
"Come unto Me ... I will give you rest" ... you shall find rest Matthew 11:28-29	
Emotional Pain	Jesus Words of Comfort

Freedom from Sin

The spiritual sin issues, bitterness, temporal values, rebellion, pride, moral failure, deception, and hypocrisy are resolvable due to the fact that the heart's wounds are healed and needs have been met. These are definitions and evidences of spiritual sin issues.

- Bitterness is internal anger, hurt, and resentment about wrong done towards self or others. Evidences of bitterness are mistrust and resentment of people, depression, insensitivity, ungratefulness, criticism, retaliation, and also gossip.

- Temporal Values is placing a higher value on personal goals, position, or possessions than on relationships in our lives. Temporal values can consume our days and time with attaining personal goals, position, or possessions to the damage of relationships. Focusing on our personal rights, needs, and goals, and damaging others to accomplish those goals, needs, and rights.

- *Rebellion* is an act of defying an established authority. Choosing one's own desires instead of staying within the boundaries set by authority. Evidence of a rebellious person is rationalizing wrong behavior, not listening and heeding to counsel, and causing others to take offense of those in authority. Challenging all persons of authority.

- Pride is a focus on exalting self and a belief that one is above others. Also, an attitude of self-sufficiency and independence. Being concerned with position and believing that position is accomplished only through one's own abilities and actions. Evidences of pride are desiring to be recognized and appreciated and feeling hurt when others are instead. Quick judgment of failures in others, becoming defensive when corrected or criticized, and having difficulty admitting when wrong. Talking most often about self in conversations, focusing on my knowledge and experience, believing my success is self-made. Unable to listen to another speak without cutting in on the person.

- Obvious Pride is focusing on one's self, one's possessions, one's goals, or one's achievements.

- Hidden Pride is focusing on one's inner pain and feelings of rejection leading to an inability to respond to other people's need.

- Moral Failure is meeting sexual needs through wrong means such as lust, defrauding, incest, pornography, rape, and unfaithfulness to a marriage partner. Evidences of moral failure are impure thoughts, desires, and actions. Emotionally and spiritually not being able to care for people in a relationship. Focus on a person's physical body instead of the person when interacting with the person.

- Spiritual Deception is being deceived about God. Relying on false sources spiritually to gain guidance and success in life. Evidences of spiritual deception are rebellion, moral failure, interest or participation in occult activities, religious fetishes, drugs, cursing, and pharisaical attitudes or actions.

- Hypocrisy is pretending something on the outside that is not real on the inside. To act, play a part, or pretend to be someone else. Projecting an outward image that is false. Evidences of hypocrisy are not being open with others but staying on the surface relationally. Secretly doing wrong, but pretending to be a good, moral person. Pretending to be submissive, without problems, covering up wrong actions by outwardly being conservative, lying to cover up truth, and doing religious activity only to be seen and praised by others. Giving money or gifts for the admiration of people. Praying, fasting, or serving to gain acceptance from the Christian community and to impress others.

Resolving emotional and abusive issues cause these spiritual issues to not be needed any longer. Involvement in these spiritual issues opens a gate for the enemy to come into the heart and life of a person and gain control over the person. This door can also be opened by a person who is in or has been given authority over you, such as your parents, teachers, babysitters, doctors, and church leaders. In order to resolve this and remove the enemy, one must acknowledge the sin they have participated in, or that the one in authority participated in, confess to God that sin, renounce the sin, abandon the right to have needs met in a sinful way, and ask God to forgive the sin. The heart is the seat of the emotions. Forgiveness of others must come from the heart. This means you must allow yourself to feel the pain you experienced when the damage took place. Ask Jesus to aid you in feeling the pain, and as you begin to feel the painful memory, ask Him to remove the pain from your heart. This process cannot be done quickly or unemotionally. Jesus promised to restore our souls. Ask Him to guide your restoration and healing process. Make lists of those—family members, friends, employers, teachers, church situations, peers, spouses, children, God, and even yourself—that have damaged you. Pray through each instance, no matter how insignificant you may think they are to your heart. Here is a list of sin issues and prayers that will aid in resolving sin and the enemy's control in ones heart and life in each spiritual area.

- Bitterness: "Lord, I acknowledge that I have developed resentment and anger toward others who have hurt me. This has caused me to experience inner pain and to build walls between others and myself. I choose to forgive each individual by name who has hurt me. I am willing to allow Jesus to pay for the emotional pain they caused me. Lord, reveal to me those areas of bitterness, resentment, and anger within me that have been buried for so long. I want to identify and resolve each one of them. Lord Jesus, I ask You to take back the ground I gave to the enemy through my bitterness, and I yield that ground to Your control, in the name of Jesus."

- Temporal Values: "Lord, I acknowledge that I have placed other things and myself as a priority above both You and those I am in relationship with. I choose to make You first in my life and to establish priorities that honor You. I ask You to reveal to me each area that I have given value above You and others. I choose to place relationship with You and others as a priority above my own goals, power, position, possessions, rights, and needs. I have placed a higher value on _____ _____ to the neglect of my relationships. I ask Your forgiveness. Lord Jesus, I ask You to take back the ground in my heart and life that I gave to the enemy through having temporal values, and I yield that ground to Your control, in the name of Jesus."

- Rebellion: "Lord, I ask You to reveal to me each area of rebellion that I have demonstrated toward those in authority over me. I want to respond with an open heart and a submissive attitude toward each person You have placed over me. Show me those people whose authority I should not place over myself. Forgive my rebellion toward parents, spouses, employers, government, spiritual leaders, and also toward You, God. I acknowledge my rebellious attitude towards _____ _____ by responding with a humble attitude. I choose to submit to Your authority through this person, in the name of Jesus."

- Pride: "Lord, I acknowledge attitudes of pride in my heart. I have focused primarily on my rights, interests, needs, desires, and goals. I have neglected to place You first in my life. I ask You to open my heart so that I can respond in humility and recognition of who You are. Also, open my heart to love and care for the needs of people around me and cause me to esteem them better than myself. I choose to humble myself and acknowledge the evidence of pride through my self-focus. I ask You to take back the ground in my life given to the enemy through each area of pride, and I yield that ground to Your control, in the name of Jesus."

- Moral Failure: "Lord, I acknowledge that I have yielded to sinful activities to meet my own sexual needs. This has brought to me guilt, shame, and distance from You. I want Your cleansing so that I can be free from the enslavement of moral sin. Reveal to me each way I have violated Your moral principles in my desires, thoughts, and actions. I choose to forgive myself for each of these areas causing me to experience guilt and the consequences of my sin. I am willing to accept the emotional pain and consequences I have caused myself. I have given ground to the enemy in my life through sinful desires, thoughts, and actions. I acknowledge and renounce each specific moral failure and ask You to break that stronghold in my heart and life. I ask You to take back the ground I have given to the enemy through my involvement, and I yield that ground to Your control, in the name of Jesus."

Upon concluding this prayer, ask Jesus to give a picture that shows you that you are morally clean. If you do not get a picture, ask Jesus if there is anything more He knows of that you need to acknowledge. If there is, He will remind you of what it is and then pray through the instance he has shown you. Then afterwards, ask once again if you are morally clean.

- Spiritual Deception: "Lord, I acknowledge, that I have given ground to the enemy by relying on false sources to give guidance, to satisfy my needs, and to find success in life. I confess and renounce each area in which I have allowed the enemy to influence me. Lord, I confess that I or generations of my family have participated in personal occult activities and the use of illegal drugs. I ask Your forgiveness and renounce each activity by name. I ask You, Lord Jesus, to take back the ground that I or my family gave to the enemy, and I yield that ground to Your control. I ask that You would break any bondage this involvement would have on my children, in the name of Jesus."

- Hypocrisy: " Lord, I recognize that I have not been truthful in my relationship with You and others. I have projected an outward image that is false. I have performed to receive the acceptance and praise of people. I have pretended to be good and morally right while hiding secret sins and wrong attitudes in my heart. I choose now to be totally honest, open, and truthful with You and others. I now acknowledge my hypocrisy as evidenced through, (list the areas). I confess my weaknesses. I choose to be transparent with you and others. I ask Your forgiveness for my hypocrisy. I ask You, Lord Jesus, to take back the ground I have given over to the enemy in my heart and life by my hypocrisy. I ask You to reveal all the areas of hypocrisy that might be hidden or that I am blind to seeing. I give this ground over to Your control, in the name of Jesus."

Steps toward Healing the Heart

EPILOGUE

What good would this book be if you, the reader, would not be able to use it as a tool to find healing or help someone else come to healing? Therefore, the following charts and steps of information will help guide you to seek your own healing by coming to Jesus. Give your heart to Jesus—invite Him into the infected and diseased places of your heart that need healing.

STEP 1:

Define the emotional pain you feel when you find yourself reacting. Use the emotional pain word list included as Chart 6. Circle each pain word that you have ever felt on a regular basis growing up or in a difficult time.

Emotional Pain Words

Abandoned	Destroyed	Insensitive to my needs	Separated
Accused	Detested	Insignificant	Shamed
Afraid	Devalued	Invalidated	Silenced
All my fault	Didn't belong	Isolated	Stepped on
Alone	Didn't measure up	Knocked down	Shattered
Always wrong	Dirty	Judged	Stressed
Angry	Disappointed	Left out	Stupid
Annihilated	Discarded	Lied to	Suicidal
Anxious	Discouraged	Lonely	Taken advantage of
Apathetic	Disgraced	Lost	Terrified
Ashamed	Dishonored	Made fun of	Threatened
Avoided	Disregarded	Manipulated	Torn apart
Awkward	Disrespected	Mistreated	Trapped
Babied	Dominated	Misunderstood	Trashed
Bad	Embarrassed	Mocked	Tricked
Belittled	Empty	Molested	Ugly
Betrayed	Excluded	Neglected	Unable to speak
Bewildered	Exhausted	No good	Unaccepted
Bitter	Exploited	No support	Uncaring
Blamed	Exposed	No way out	Uncared for
Can't do anything right	Failure	Not being affirmed	Unchosen
Can't trust anyone	Fear, fearful	Not cared for	Underdesireable
Cheap	Foolish	Not cherished	Unfairly judged
Cheated	Forced	Not deserving to live	Unfairly treated
Coerced	Forsaken	Not listened to	Unfit
Condemned	Friendless	Not measure up	Unimportant
Confused	Frightened	Not valued	Unheard
Conspired against	Frustrated	Opinions not valued	Unloved
Controlled	Good for nothing	Overwhelmed	Unlovable
Cornered	Guilty	Paralyzed	Unnecessary
Crushed	Hated	Powerless	Unneeded
Cursed	Hate myself	Pressured	Unnoticed
Cut off	Helpless	Pressure to perfom	Unprotected
Deceived	Hopeless	Publicly shamed	Unreponsive
Defeated	Humiliated	Put down	Unsafe
Defenseless	Hurt	Rejected	Unwanted
Defrauded	Hysterical	Repulsed	Useless
Degraded	Ignored	Resentful	Valueless
Depressed	Impure	Revenge	Violated
Deprived	Inadequate	Ridiculed	Vulnerable
Deserted	Incompetent	Ruined	Walked on
Desires rejected	Indecent	Sad	Wasted
Despair	Inferior	Scared	Weak
Despised	Inhibited	Secluded	Worthless
Despondent	Insecure	Self disgusted	Wounded

STEP 2:

In Chart 7, combine together the pain words you circled on the word list, which mean the same to you or are in the same category of pain. For instance, defenseless, helpless, unprotected, or abused could be a group of words combined that mean the same. My first group of words I circled and combined was: abandoned, rejected, betrayed, left behind, un-chosen, and alone. I put these words in my first box.

Identifying One's Emotional Pain		
Category of pain	Category of pain	Category of pain
Category of pain	Category of pain	Category of pain

Identifying One's Emotional Pain		
Category of pain	Category of pain	Category of pain
Category of pain	Category of pain	Category of pain

STEP 3:

On Chart 7, each box of combined words should have a category of pain. I wrote rejection as the category of my pain. As the cause of pain, I wrote, "Abandonment by nine sets of parents." My next box of words was, "Defenseless, unprotected, traumatic fear, and abused." The category of pain was fear. The cause of pain was punishment and abuse. You may also use the following charts to help formulate the causes and categories of emotional pain and damage done to your heart. If you seem to be doing okay, go on to Chart 14, step 4. Just as an encouragement, I had to do chart 14 several times before I was satisfied with the finished analysis. Chart 15 is an example of my Chart 14 that is completed.

Family Members Who Have Hurt Me		
	Release	Pay
List each family member who has hurt you in the past.	How did they hurt you? (List Issues)	Describe the emotional pain caused by the hurt.
Father		
Mother		

Step-parents		
Siblings		
Others		
Friends		
Teachers, Students, Classroom experiences		
Employer, Employee		

Belivers, Church situations, pastor, leader, etc.		
God (List the ways you think God has hurt you)		
Myself (list each area for which you cannot forgive yourself.)		
others		

"Lord, I choose to forgive _____ for _____ causing me to feel _____ and I am willing to pay for the emotional pain and consequenses that _____ has caused me. I ask You Lord Jesus, to take back the ground I gave to the enemy through my bitterness and I yield that ground to Your control.

My Spouse Who Has Hurt Me	
Release	Pay
Define each way your spouse has hurt you in the past.	Describe the emotional pain you feel because of the hurt.
1.	
2.	
3.	
4.	
5.	
6.	
7.	
8.	
9.	
10.	

"Lord, I choose to forgive _____ for _____ causing me to feel _____ and I am willing to pay for the emotional pain and consequenses that _____ has caused me. I ask You Lord Jesus, to take back the ground I gave to the enemy through my bitterness and I yield that ground to Your control.

Emotional, Physical, and Spiritual Abuse			
List each person who abused you, the way you were abused, and the emotional pain it caused.			
	Person	Describe Abuse	Emotional pain
Emotional Abuse			
Physical Abuse			
Spiritual Abuse			

"Lord, I acknowledge and renounce the _____ that _____ perpetrated against me and ask You to break the stronghold in my life. I ask You, Lord Jesus, to take back the ground given to the enemy through the abuse and I yield that ground to Your control.

"Lord, I choose to forgive _____ for _____ causing me to feel _____ and I am willing to pay the emotional pain and consequences that _____ has caused me."

Emotional Pain Words Associated with Sexual Abuse

Check each of the following emotional pain words you have felt.

- ☐ Alone
- ☐ Afraid
- ☐ Angry
- ☐ Anxious
- ☐ Bad
- ☐ Belittled
- ☐ Confused
- ☐ Controlled
- ☐ Couldn't Trust Anyone
- ☐ Deceived
- ☐ Defenseless
- ☐ Destroyed
- ☐ Dominated
- ☐ Dirty
- ☐ Devalued
- ☐ Disrespected
- ☐ Disgusting
- ☐ Embarrassed
- ☐ Exposed
- ☐ Forced
- ☐ Frustrated
- ☐ Gross
- ☐ Guilty
- ☐ Hateful
- ☐ Helpless
- ☐ Hollow
- ☐ Other Feelings

- ☐ Hurt
- ☐ Inferior
- ☐ Inadequate
- ☐ Invalidated
- ☐ Manipulated
- ☐ Molested
- ☐ No Way Out
- ☐ Not Cherished
- ☐ Not Good Enough
- ☐ Out of Control
- ☐ Overwhelmed
- ☐ Pressured
- ☐ Repulsed
- ☐ Ruined
- ☐ Sad
- ☐ Scared
- ☐ Secluded
- ☐ Shamed
- ☐ Suffocated
- ☐ Trapped
- ☐ Trashed; Trash
- ☐ Used
- ☐ Unable to Speak
- ☐ Unsafe
- ☐ Violated
- ☐ Vulnerable

_____

_____

_____

_____

Sexual Abuse		
List each time you were abused or taken advantage of and the emotional pain it caused		
	Individual	Emotional Pain
fondled		
Incest		
Sexual Abuse		
Rape		
Forced Abortion		
Forced Defrauding		
Forced Premarital sexual Relationship		

Forced Homosexuality		
Sexaul Harassment		

"Lord, I acknowledge and renounce the _____ that _____ perpetrated against me and ask You to break the stronghold in my life. I ask You, Lord Jesus, to take back the ground given to the enemy through the abuse and I yield that ground to Your control.

"Lord, I choose to forgive _____ for _____ causing me to feel _____ and I am willing to pay the emotional pain and consequences that _____ has caused me."

STEP 4:

Using Chart 14 list the categories of pain you wrote out on Chart 7. List these under (*emotional pain felt*). Also on Chart 14, list causes of your pain or the life experiences that contributed to you feeling the pain words. For instance, I felt the pain of abandonment, rejection, betrayal, being left behind, not chosen, and alone. My contributing experience or life factor was the nine times I was abandoned by parents and left behind for good. My second life factor was the abuse and punishment I endured, which caused me to feel the pain words of fear and unprotected. There may be several life experiences that caused you to feel the pain words. List all of the experiences that come to your memory. Then ask Jesus if there are any you have forgotten that He wants you to remember at this time.

Contributing Life Factors	
Contributing Life Factors that Caused Pain	Emotional Pain Categories

Emotional Core Life Issues:

Core Damage Statement	Core Care Statement

My chart of emotional core life issues is written out as a help for you. As you can see, my Core Emotional Issues are: rejection, humiliation, fear, abuse, and trauma. These are the areas in which the enemy has and still tries to attack me in my life. These are the areas in which God shows Himself strong and able to destroy the works of the enemy.

Birdie's Contributing Life Factors	
Contributing Life Factors that Caused Pain	Emotional Pain Categories
No explanations given	Emotional Neglect
other children being chosen	Replaced & Rejection
Traumatic physical abuse and punishment	Fear, Trauma, and panic
Prarents leaving, sisters being taken away	Betrayal and abandonment
Emotional Core Life Issues:	
Rejection/Panic	
Replaced/Fear	
Neglect in preventing abuse	
Core Damage Statement	Core Care Statement
A little girl was damaged by emotional neglect and abandonment, along with no attention. She was rejected by 9 sets of parents. She was spiritually, physically, and sexually abused, and humiliated in the homes where she lived. This all created a world of fear, betrayal and lonely survival.	What if I, (care partner), cared for a little damaged girl by emotionally caring for her heart, providing her attention that would cause her to live in a world of safety and gentleness. Assuring her of his commitment to stay with her and honor her. Being someone she can trust.

STEP 5:

The Core Damage Statement is taking all categories of pain words and writing out a damage statement of the person's heart. Here is my example: "Birdie, as a little girl, was damaged by emotional neglect, abandonment, rejection, and betrayal by 9 sets of parents. This little girl was spiritually, physically, and sexually abused and humiliated in the homes she lived in, which created a world of fear, betrayal, and lonely survival."

I had circled almost all of the emotional pain words, but I put them in categories and then narrowed down the pain into one core word per category. So in my damage statement I only wrote out each category's main word. My main category words were neglect, abandonment, alone, rejection, betrayal, fear, and spiritual, physical, and sexual abuse. Here is the chart to help you write out the categories.

STEP 6:

The Core Care Statement is written by the support care person, counselor, or spouse. It is a statement of how they are going to care for the damage in the person's heart. Dan, my husband, was my care partner and this is his statement of care for me: "How about if I cared for a little damaged girl by emotionally caring for her heart, providing her the needed attention that would cause her to live in a world of safety and gentleness, assuring her of my commitment to stay with her, to honor her, and be someone she can trust." My heart was so touched as he read this to me. It met the need of my heart. He was caring for me in the areas I had been damaged. There are many other materials to help you that are available from the Caring For The Heart Ministry. You will find these materials at; www.caringfortheheart.com.

STEP 7

Resolving the issues of pain comes through taking every instance in which you were abandoned, rejected, and betrayed to Jesus in prayer conversation and asking Him to do several things. First, to give you a word picture of how the abandonment, rejections, and betrayal damaged your heart. Jesus showed me a picture of a bullwhip hitting my heart over and over again, leaving many wounds and scars. Second, as Jesus shows the pain and damage you experienced, you begin to feel the pain in your heart and you might start to cry. At this moment, ask Jesus to bring peace into your heart. Third, ask Jesus if He would be willing to heal your heart of the damage. Jesus will respond with a word picture, a verse, a song, or something that will bring comfort and peace to your heart. He showed me that He too had been hit over and over again with a whip and had also been abandoned, rejected, and betrayed by those closest to Him. Even His own Father turned His face away from Him on the cross. Fourth, Jesus then asked me if I would by name, forgive each person who abandoned, rejected or betrayed me. Take the list of people and instances from your charts and pray the following prayer through each situation or person who caused the pain.

> "Jesus, _____ (*person who damaged you*) abandoned, rejected, and betrayed me when they _____ (*damage done by them to you*). I choose by my will to forgive _____ , and I ask You, Jesus, to take the pain from my heart. Jesus, I renounce the

control the enemy has had in my heart because of my unforgiveness, bitterness, or rebellion. I now turn over control of that area of my heart to You."

Fifth, ask Jesus to show you how to respond in the future when someone abandons, rejects, or betrays you. Ask for a safe place where you can go with Jesus whenever someone seeks to damage you in this area of pain. In time, Jesus may show you other situations you need to bring to Him in prayer. His timing and processes in your life are always perfect.

When caring for someone else, always seek to accept, understand, and care for the pain they have experienced. Get an understanding of the repeated areas where they have been damaged and continued to feel the pain. Use the opposite of the emotional pain word they have circled and use it in a positive statement to begin caring for the individual. For example, if your wife or child was emotionally neglected, ask her if she would allow you to begin to care for her by giving her your attention. Ask questions about their pain and begin focusing on caring about their feelings of neglect. Putting yourself in their shoes and looking at the pain through their eyes will enable you to come alongside them in humility and unconditional love. If you are intellectually locked in your own heart, do not try to minister to people who are damaged. You will not be able to empathize with them and could do worse damage to them. Find help in why you are intellectually locked in your heart. A good sign that you are locked is if you hardly ever show emotion, even when you are alone in private.

This concludes my story and how my heart was able to overcome the world and all that happened to me. I found a dear friend in Jesus. He gave me a new heart and life. I came into relationship with a God who is my Father. I am able to give and receive love. I do still go through trials in life. The difference now is that I know where to go when my heart is overwhelmed. I pray that after reading my story, you will be enabled to come to Jesus and give Him your heart. You may come to freedom through a love relationship with Father God. Come, give Him your heart. From this dark world, let Him draw you apart. The Father is speaking so tenderly. *Give Him Your Heart.*

BIBLIOGRAPHY

1. Hewitt, E.E., *"Give Me Thy Heart," Heart Songs*. Boston: Chapple Publishing Company, Ltd, 1909.

2. Whithall Smith, Hannah. *The Christian's Secret of a Happy Life*. Uhrichsville, OH: Barbour Books, 1998.

3. Gilliam Bill, ED.E,. *Lifetime Guarantee: Making Your Christian Life Work and What to do When it Doesn't*. Brentwood, TN Wolegemuth and Hyatt Publishers, Inc., 1990.

4. Crosby, Dr. Stephen. *Silent Killers of the Faith*. Shippensburg, PA: Treasure House - Destiny Image Publishers, Inc., 2004.

5. Regier, John. Charts # 3 - 15 used by permission. Colorado Springs: John Regier - Caring for the Heart Ministries, 2007©. http://www.caringfortheheart. com, design, A Tier One, 2006

6. Regier, John. *Biblical Concepts Counseling Workbook*. Colorado Springs: John Regier, 1999© http://www.caringfortheheart.com, design, A Tier One, 2006

7. All names and pronouns of the Triune God are capitalized within the text.